WINTER WARRIOR

A VIETNAM VET'S ANTI-WAR ODYSSEY

EVE GILBERT

FANTAGRAPHICS BOOKS

For Ricky, and Thinking for Yourself.

Eve Darling Gilbert is a cartoonist, illustrator and
painter. She lives in New Jersey with her husband
and her plants. You can find more of her work,
plus paintings, at www.evegilbert.com.

Book Design: Jacob Covey
Editor: Conrad Groth
Proofreader: Christina Hwang
Production: Preston White
Associate Publisher: Eric Reynolds
Publisher: Gary Groth

Fantagraphics Books, Inc.
7563 Lake City Way NE
Seattle, WA 98115

ISBN: 978-1-68396-213-7
Library of Congress Control Number: 2018967047
First Fantagraphics Books edition: 2019
Printed in China

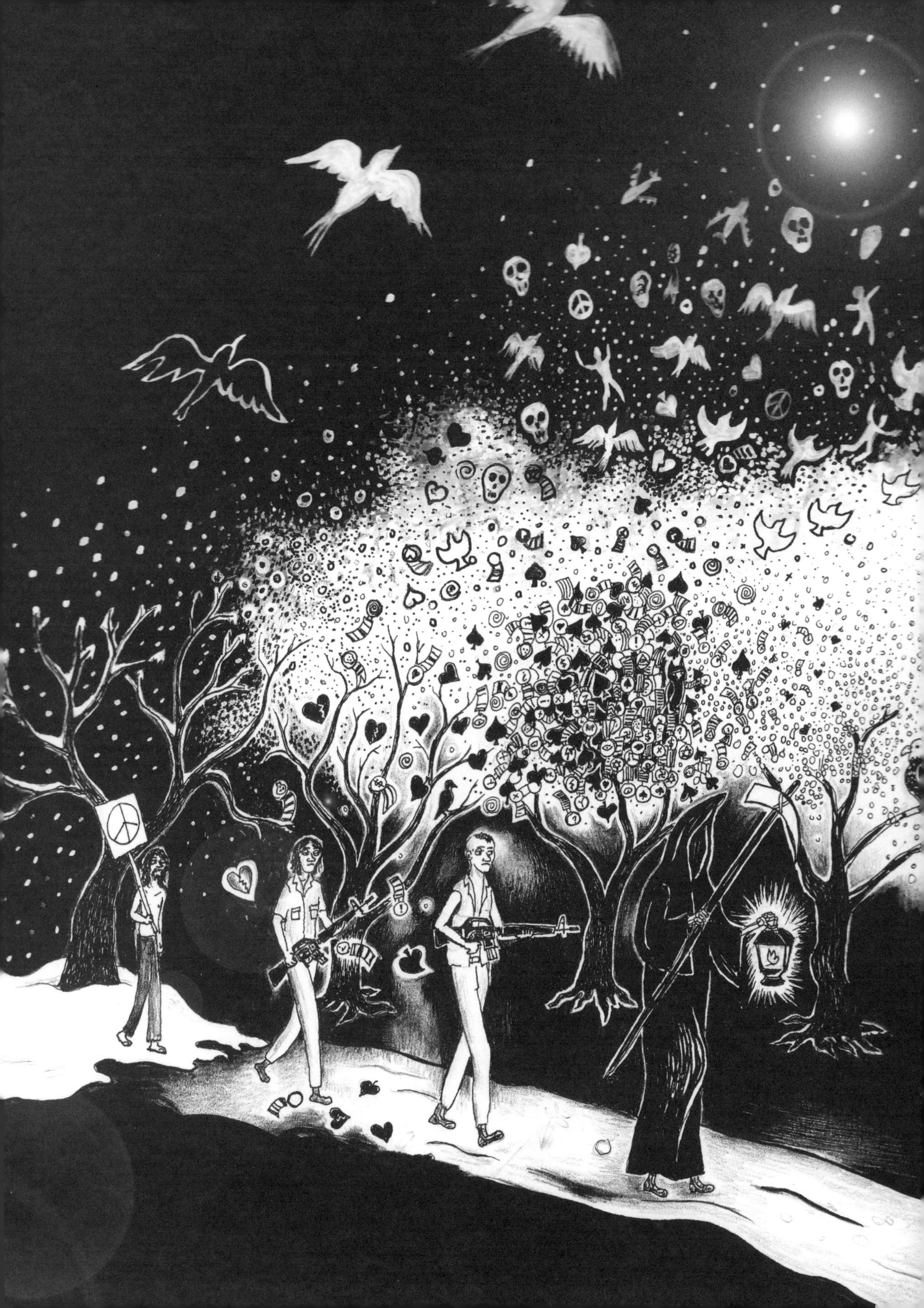

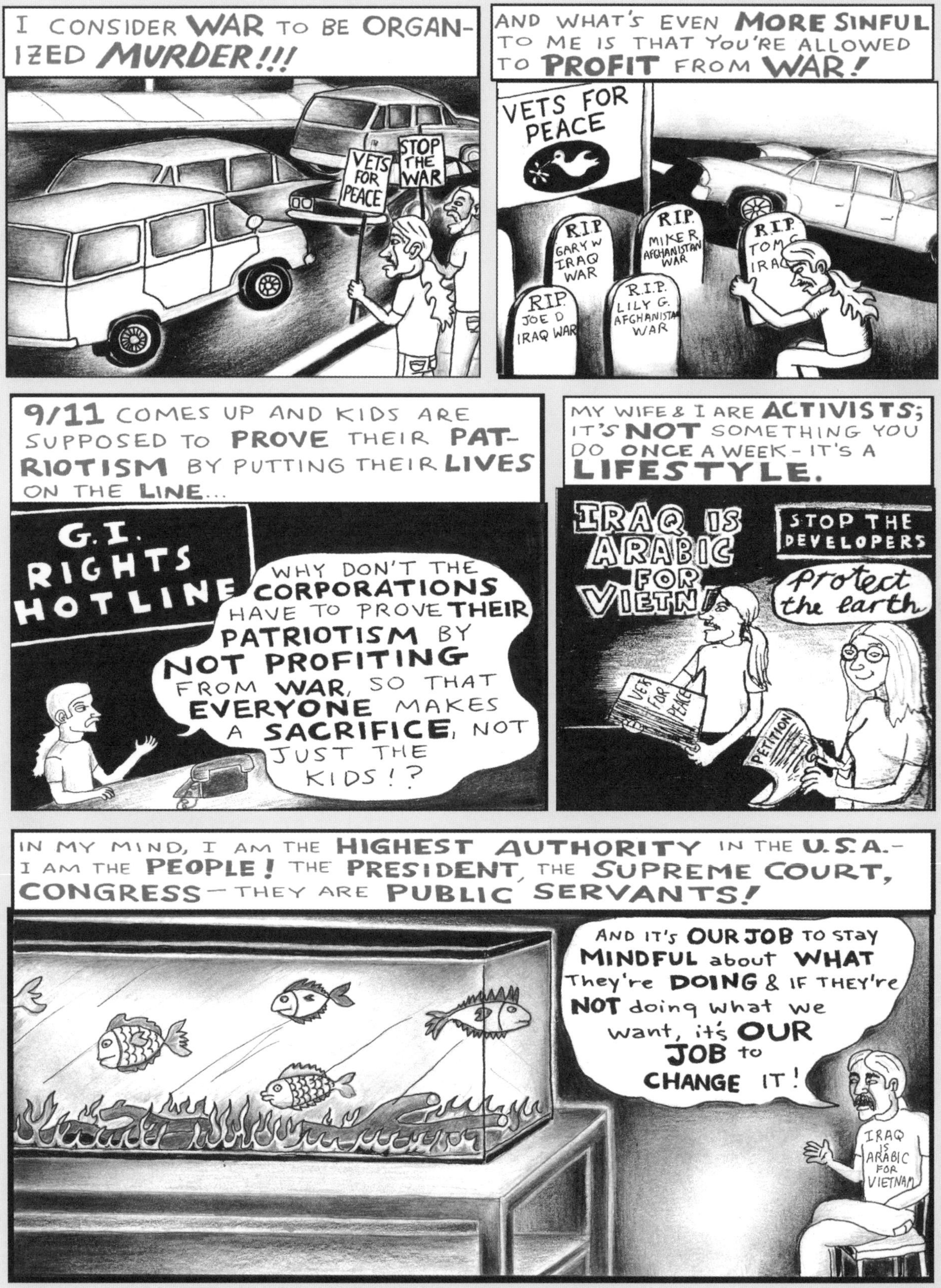
I CONSIDER WAR TO BE ORGANIZED MURDER!!!
VETS FOR PEACE
STOP THE WAR
AND WHAT'S EVEN MORE SINFUL TO ME IS THAT YOU'RE ALLOWED TO PROFIT FROM WAR!
VETS FOR PEACE
R.I.P. GARY W IRAQ WAR
R.I.P. MIKE R. AFGHANISTAN WAR
R.I.P. JOE D IRAQ WAR
R.I.P. LILY G. AFGHANISTAN WAR
9/11 COMES UP AND KIDS ARE SUPPOSED TO PROVE THEIR PATRIOTISM BY PUTTING THEIR LIVES ON THE LINE...
G.I. RIGHTS HOTLINE
WHY DON'T THE CORPORATIONS HAVE TO PROVE THEIR PATRIOTISM BY NOT PROFITING FROM WAR, SO THAT EVERYONE MAKES A SACRIFICE, NOT JUST THE KIDS!?
MY WIFE & I ARE ACTIVISTS; IT'S NOT SOMETHING YOU DO ONCE A WEEK - IT'S A LIFESTYLE.
STOP THE DEVELOPERS
Protect the earth
PETITION
IN MY MIND, I AM THE HIGHEST AUTHORITY IN THE U.S.A. - I AM THE PEOPLE! THE PRESIDENT, THE SUPREME COURT, CONGRESS - THEY ARE PUBLIC SERVANTS!
AND IT'S OUR JOB to stay MINDFUL about WHAT They're DOING & IF THEY're NOT doing what we want, it's OUR JOB to CHANGE IT!
IRAQ IS ARABIC FOR VIETNAM

WHEN WE HAVE A **DEMONSTRATION** AGAINST THE **WAR** TODAY, NO **STUDENTS** SHOW UP - IT'S JUST US **OLDER PEOPLE.**

I THINK WHAT **HAPPENED** WAS SO **MANY PEOPLE** STARTED **STANDING UP** FOR THEIR **RIGHTS** THAT THEY **QUIT** TEACHING **CIVICS** IN **SCHOOL.**

THEY CUT **MONEY** FROM PUBLIC EDUCATION & THE **RICH** PEOPLE WHO **RUN** THE **FUCKING SHOW,** T H E I R KIDS GO TO **COLLEGE.**

AND THE **POOR** PEOPLE WILL **SERVE** IN A **FUCKING BURGER KING!**

I COME FROM A **WORKING CLASS** FAMILY - MY MOM MARRIED A MAN NAMED **CAMIL** & WE MOVED TO **HIALEAH, FLORIDA.**

HIALEAH WAS WHERE ALL THE **POOR PEOPLE** LIVED; MY PARENTS HAD TROUBLE PAYING **RENT** & A LOT OF NIGHTS WE WENT TO BED WITHOUT **FOOD**.

MY REAL FATHER, HIS NAME WAS **ABRAMSON**; HE WAS IN THE **ARMY AIR CORPS** IN **WWⅡ** & HE GAVE ME THESE **MEDALS**.

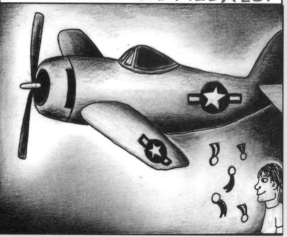

GROWING UP, YOU **PLAY WAR**. AND I HAD HIS **MEDALS** & HIS **HAT**.

MEDALS WERE HOW I BELIEVED MY **MANHOOD** WOULD BE MEASURED.

I WAS GONNA BE A MARINE AND WIN A BUNCH OF FUCKING MEDALS!

I WAS **TAUGHT** THAT **AMERICA** WAS THE **BEST COUNTRY** & **GOD** WAS ON **OUR SIDE** & IT WAS **OK** TO GO AROUND **FREEING PEOPLE**.

THE MOST **EVIL** THING YOU COULD **BE** WAS A **COMMUNIST**. ON **T.V.**, YOU WOULD SEE A **MAP** AND IT WOULD BE TURNING **RED** WITH THE **COMMUNISM SPREADING**.

IN SCHOOL, WE HAD **AIR RAID DRILLS** AND WE WOULD **HIDE** UNDER OUR DESKS.

MY **STEPFATHER** WAS IN THE **JOHN BIRCH SOCIETY**... HIS **JOB** WAS TO MAKE **TAPES** ABOUT THE **COMMUNIST CONSPIRACY**.

HE WAS A **COP**... AND A **BULLY**. HE **BEAT** ME, MY **MOTHER** AND MY **SISTER** ALL THE TIME.

PEOPLE DID NOT LIKE US BECAUSE WE WERE **JEWISH**. IN **JUNIOR HIGH**, I STARTED GETTING **JUMPED** AFTER SCHOOL.

SO I MADE A **DECISION** THAT AS LONG AS I WAS GETTING MY **ASS KICKED** ANYWAY, I WOULD GET MY ASS KICKED **FIGHTING BACK**. ONCE I STARTED **FIGHTING BACK**, EVERYTHING **CHANGED**.

I BECAME A **DISCIPLINE** PROBLEM. I GOT INTO **FIGHTS** IN THE HALLWAY, I **SKIPPED** SCHOOL, I **HIT** MY **TEACHER**.

I WAS IN A GROUP YOU PROBABLY WOULD'VE CALLED THE **GREASERS**. YOU HAD TO SMOKE **CIGARETTES**, DRINK **ALCOHOL** & YOU HAD TO **FIGHT**.

LET'S GO **BEAT UP** SOME **CUBANS!**

Then we can go get **DRUNK!**

OR get **DRUNK** & Then **BEAT** the **CUBANS!**

I JUST DIDN'T **DO WELL** WITH **AUTHORITY**... I GOT **ARRESTED** SEVERAL TIMES.

Hialeah

SO MY **GRANDFATHER** WORKED OUT THIS **DEAL** WITH THE **JUDGE** – THEY AGREED TO **HOLD** MY **RECORD**, AND I AGREED TO **ENLIST**.

YOUR **HONOR**... my Grandson could be an **ASSET** to the **COMMUNITY** IF he would be allowed to **SERVE** in the **MILITARY**.

JUST US

YOU / US

HONORABLE WANKER MAN

I WILL **HOLD** his **RECORD** IF he **AGREES** to **ENLIST** after **GRADUATION!**

WHEN THE **MARINE RECRUITERS** CAME TO MY SCHOOL, ALL THE **GIRLS** THAT I **WANTED TO FUCK** – THEY LIKED THE GUYS IN THOSE **UNIFORMS**.

MARINE CORPS BUILDS MEN

ENLIST NOW!

I'M GONNA GET THAT **UNIFORM** & THOSE **MEDALS** & all those **GIRLS** will wanna **FUCK ME**, too!

IF YOU GET **DRAFTED**, YOU'LL END UP IN THE **ARMY**... THE ARMY IS **SHIT**... Don't you want the **UNIFORM**? Don't you want to be a **MAN**?

SIGN ME UP!

MY **CAREER**
by Scott Camil   1965

When I graduate, I'm going to be a **MARINE**. I want to be a **MARINE** because the **MARINES** are the **TOUGHEST**. We are going to **FREE** the world from **COMMUNISM** and be **HEROES**. I'm going to win a bunch of **MEDALS**. I'll start off as a **PRIVATE** and become a **GENERAL**

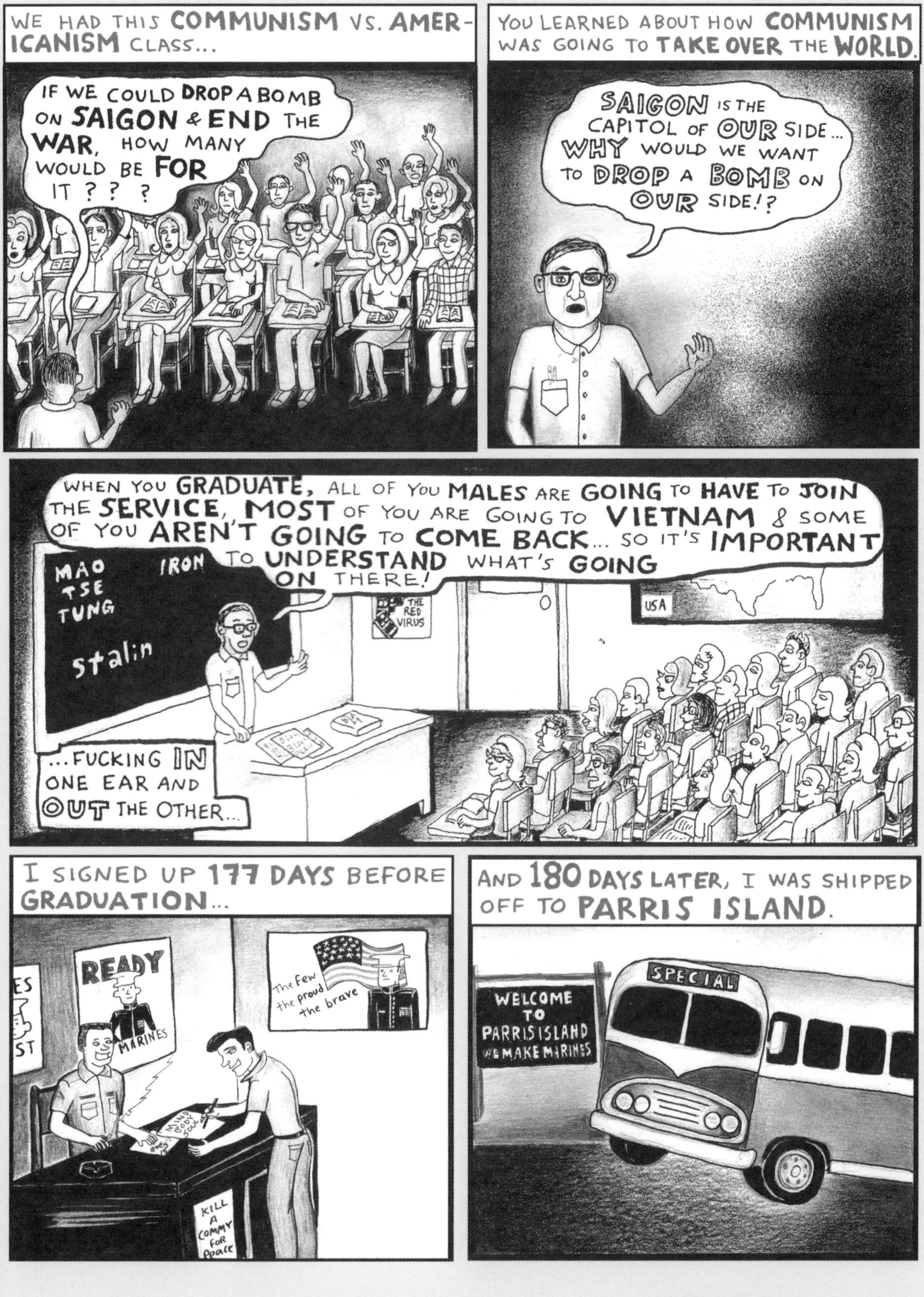

WE HAD THIS COMMUNISM VS. AMERICANISM CLASS...
IF WE COULD DROP A BOMB ON SAIGON & END THE WAR, HOW MANY WOULD BE FOR IT ? ? ?
YOU LEARNED ABOUT HOW COMMUNISM WAS GOING TO TAKE OVER THE WORLD.
SAIGON IS THE CAPITOL OF OUR SIDE... WHY WOULD WE WANT TO DROP A BOMB ON OUR SIDE!?
WHEN YOU GRADUATE, ALL OF YOU MALES ARE GOING TO HAVE TO JOIN THE SERVICE, MOST OF YOU ARE GOING TO VIETNAM & SOME OF YOU AREN'T GOING TO COME BACK... SO IT'S IMPORTANT TO UNDERSTAND WHAT'S GOING ON THERE!
MAO TSE TUNG
IRON
stalin
THE RED VIRUS
USA
...FUCKING IN ONE EAR AND OUT THE OTHER...
I SIGNED UP 177 DAYS BEFORE GRADUATION...
READY
MARINES
The few the proud the brave
MIND BODY SOUL
KILL A COMMY FOR Peace
AND 180 DAYS LATER, I WAS SHIPPED OFF TO PARRIS ISLAND.
SPECIAL
WELCOME TO PARRIS ISLAND WE MAKE MARINES

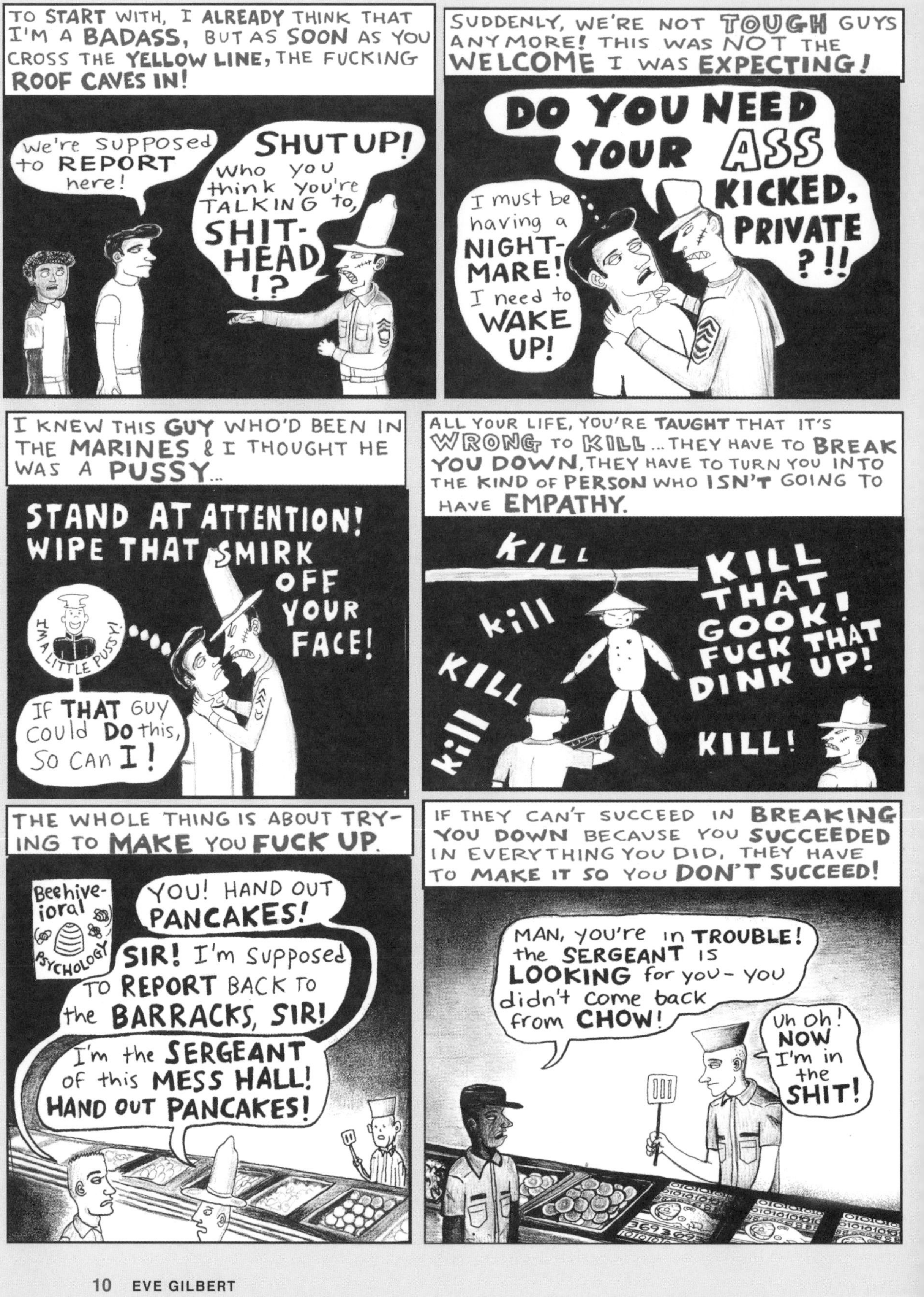

TO START WITH, I ALREADY THINK THAT I'M A BADASS, BUT AS SOON AS YOU CROSS THE YELLOW LINE, THE FUCKING ROOF CAVES IN!
We're supposed to REPORT here!
SHUT UP! Who you think you're TALKING to, SHIT-HEAD!?
SUDDENLY, WE'RE NOT TOUGH GUYS ANYMORE! THIS WAS NOT THE WELCOME I WAS EXPECTING!
DO YOU NEED YOUR ASS KICKED, PRIVATE?!!
I must be having a NIGHT-MARE! I need to WAKE UP!
I KNEW THIS GUY WHO'D BEEN IN THE MARINES & I THOUGHT HE WAS A PUSSY...
STAND AT ATTENTION! WIPE THAT SMIRK OFF YOUR FACE!
I'M A LITTLE PUSSY!
IF THAT GUY could DO this, So Can I!
ALL YOUR LIFE, YOU'RE TAUGHT THAT IT'S WRONG TO KILL... THEY HAVE TO BREAK YOU DOWN, THEY HAVE TO TURN YOU INTO THE KIND OF PERSON WHO ISN'T GOING TO HAVE EMPATHY.
KILL
kill
KILL
kill
KILL THAT GOOK! FUCK THAT DINK UP!
KILL!
THE WHOLE THING IS ABOUT TRY-ING TO MAKE YOU FUCK UP.
Beehive-ioral PSYCHOLOGY
YOU! HAND OUT PANCAKES!
SIR! I'm supposed TO REPORT BACK TO the BARRACKS, SIR!
I'm the SERGEANT of this MESS HALL! HAND OUT PANCAKES!
IF THEY CAN'T SUCCEED IN BREAKING YOU DOWN BECAUSE YOU SUCCEEDED IN EVERYTHING YOU DID, THEY HAVE TO MAKE IT SO YOU DON'T SUCCEED!
MAN, you're in TROUBLE! the SERGEANT is LOOKING for you- you didn't come back from CHOW!
Uh Oh! NOW I'm in the SHIT!

FROM **PARRIS ISLAND**, I WENT TO **CAMP GEIGER** FOR **INFANTRY TRAINING** & THEN **CAMP LEJEUNE**.

THE **COMMUNISTS** WERE TRYING TO **TAKE OVER** THE **WORLD** & WE HAD TO **GO OVER THERE** & **STOP** THEM BEFORE THEY CAME **HERE!**

VIETNAM

I WOULDN'T HAVE BEEN **ABLE** TO TELL YOU WHAT A **COMMUNIST** WAS... BUT I WANTED TO SEE WHAT IT **FELT** LIKE TO **KILL** A PERSON. I WANTED TO SEE IF, DURING THE **HEAT** OF **BATTLE**, I WOULD BE A **MAN!**

PRIVATE CAMIL, REPORTING FOR **DUTY!**

ALPHA-NORTH 1/11 MARINES

MARCH 20. 1966

WHERE YOU **FROM?!**

FLORIDA! YOU GOTTA **TALK** TO **MAIN!** He's from Florida, too!

HIALEAH, FLORIDA!

MAIN BECAME MY **FIRST FRIEND** IN **VIETNAM.**

I'M SCOTT, I'M FROM **HIALEAH!**

FLORIDA!? I'M FROM **JACKSONVILLE!**

I LIKE THE **GIRLS** IN **JACKSONVILLE!**

SLAP!

NEW PEOPLE EITHER GOT **GUARD DUTY** OR **MESS DUTY** — SO I GOT **GUARD DUTY.**

DO NOT LOAD THE WEAPON WITHOUT **PERMISSION** ... IF YOU **SEE** something, call the **GUARD SHACK** & **WAIT** FOR **PERMISSION!**

WHAT IS HE, **NUTS!?** I'M IN **FUCKING VIETNAM!!!** IF WE GET **ATTACKED, MY GUN** IS GONNA BE **LOADED!**

I'M **NOT** WAITING FOR **PERMISSION!**

US MARINE

3 WEEKS IN COUNTRY, A TRIP FLARE ON THE WIRE WENT OFF...THEY WERE ALREADY **INSIDE THE WIRE!**

I WAS THE **FIRST ONE** FROM OUR BASE WHO **FIRED**...I'M GOING TO SAY IT'S BECAUSE I **THINK** FOR **MYSELF**, OTHERS ARE GOING TO SAY THAT I **DON'T FOLLOW DIRECTIONS!**

ALL OF A SUDDEN, EVERYTHING'S **BLOWING UP** & ALL THESE **BULLETS** ARE **COMING DOWN!**

I SAW **MAIN'S** BUNKER **BLOW UP** FROM THE INSIDE & A **V.C.** SHOOT **HIM & CHICO!**

THERE WAS **NOTHING** I COULD **DO**—I WAS BUSY SHOOTING THE ONES ATTACKING **MY BUNKER!**

THE CAMP WAS **DESTROYED**. **5** OF US WERE **KILLED**, **28 WOUNDED**. THE **V.C.** LEFT **40 DEAD** BEHIND. THE **NEXT** MORNING, WE GOT UP AND BROUGHT THE **DEAD** UP **FRONT**.

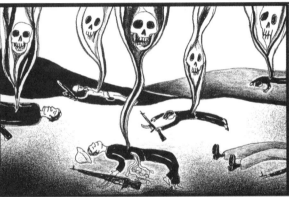

WE THREW THE **VIETNAMESE** BODIES ON THE TRUCK & **DUMPED** THEM IN THE NEXT VILLAGE— IT WAS LIKE **THROWING OUT** THE **GARBAGE**.

I PULLED OPEN **MAIN'S PONCHO** AND TOOK A **LONG, HARD** LOOK...

He's Really **DEAD!** These people want to **KILL** me... I can't make **MISTAKES** here or **I'M** really dead, **TOO!**

FROM THAT DAY ON, I WAS **RUTHLESS**. **STOPPING COMMUNISM** HAD **NOTHING** TO **DO** WITH IT ANYMORE... IT WAS **SURVIVAL**.

I'M GONNA **KILL** EVERY **MAN, WOMAN** OR **CHILD**, every **GOOK** mutherfucker that I can **KILL!**

THE NEXT THING, WE FOLLOWED **BLOOD TRAILS**... I KILLED AN **INNOCENT** PERSON LATER THAT DAY... THIS GUY HAD ON **BLACK PAJAMAS**, WORKING IN A **RICE PADDY**.

Hey **OLD MAN!** Where'd the **V.C.** GO?

Không Biết?

I DON'T UNDERSTAND

THEY SENT US THERE **WITHOUT** ANY **TRAINING** OF THE **CULTURE** OR THE **LANGUAGE**— SO WHEN WE HAD TO **INTERROGATE** PEOPLE, THEY **DON'T KNOW** WHAT THE **FUCK** WE'RE **SAYING!**

I **SAID**, Where'd the **VIET CONG** GO!!?!

IF THEY'RE NOT **ANSWERING** ME IN **ENGLISH**, THEY'RE **NOT COOPERATING**... I'M AN **ARROGANT AMERICAN**... I EXPECT EVERYONE TO **SPEAK ENGLISH**.

NEXT TIME, ANSWER ME IN **ENGLISH!**

THEY MOVED US TO THE **1st BATTALION, 1st MARINES** COMPOUND, WHERE I DID **FIRE DIRECTION CONTROL.**

① THE FORWARD OBSERVER RADIOS IN THE ENEMY'S POSITION FROM THE FIELD

② THE FDC TEAM PLOTS THE EXACT DIRECTION FOR THE OUTGOING ARTILLERY

③ THEY WOULD SHOOT THE ARTILLERY

AND IT WOULD LAND ON **TARGET!**

B LAM!

IT WAS A **105** BATTERY... WE SHOT **105 HOWITZERS.**

AT NIGHT, I'D BE ON MY RACK, LISTENING TO **ROCKET FIRE,** & THERE'S THIS **FEELING** LIKE SOMEBODY'S GONNA **PUNCH** YOU IN THE **BACK!** THAT'S **HARSH!**

screeee!!!
KA-BLAM!!!
CRASH!

IN THE **REAR,** YOU ARE A **TARGET.**

SITTING, WAITING TO GET **BOMBED— FUCK** THAT **SHIT!** I **VOLUNTEERED** TO GO OUT, **ATTACHED** TO AN **INFANTRY** UNIT SETTING UP **AMBUSHES.**

I **LIKED** DOING IT. IN A **FIREFIGHT,** I'D TAKE MY **TIME, AIM & SHOOT.**

IT WAS LIKE GOING **HUNTING** BUT THEY SUPPLIED THE **AMMO...**

WHEN I LOOKED DOWN MY **RIFLE** AND **SQUEEZED**, AND THEIR **HEADS** SPLIT OPEN LIKE A **WATERMELON**, I FELT **GOOD** INSIDE, LIKE I'D JUST ROLLED A **STRIKE** OR SANK AN **EIGHTBALL**.

TO ME, THEY WEREN'T **HUMAN**... THEY WERE **GOOKS**. AND IF THEY WERE **DEAD**, THEY **COULDN'T HURT** ME!

GUYS WOULD TIE **PRISONERS** UP, **SMASH** THEIR **TEETH, STOMP** ON THEIR **BALLS**...

YOU'RE SEEING YOUR **FRIENDS** BEING **BLOWN UP** AROUND YOU, AND EVERY **ENCOUNTER** THAT YOU HAVE, YOU HAVE THIS **BUILT-UP ANGER** INSIDE YOU.

80% OF OUR **CASUALTIES** WERE FROM **MINES** & **BOOBY TRAPS**... THERE'S **NO WAY** YOU CAN **IMAGINE** WHAT IT'S **LIKE**, FOR A **WHOLE YEAR**, EACH **STEP** COULD BE YOUR **LAST**.

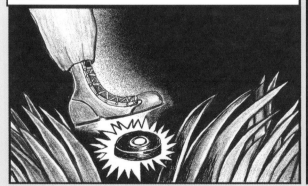

YOU WOULD SEE PEOPLE GET **BLOWN TO SHIT** & THEIR **BRAINS** WOULD **SPLATTER** ALL OVER YOU.

I'VE SEEN PEOPLE **DIE** BECAUSE THEY WEREN'T USING THEIR **BRAINS** AND PAYING **ATTENTION.** I WAS AL-WAYS **PAYING ATTENTION.**

ONCE A **V.C.** THREW A **GRENADE** AT US WHILE WE WERE OUT ON **PATROL...**

I PICKED IT UP & **THREW IT AWAY.** THEY PUT ME UP FOR A **BRONZE STAR.** I DIDN'T THINK I'D DONE ANYTHING **HEROIC** - I WAS ONLY DOING WHAT WAS **BEST FOR ME.**

I ALSO DID A **MURDER...** I WAS **TOLD** TO **KILL** THIS PERSON WHO WAS **SUPPOSED** TO BE **BAD.**

CAMIL, I NEED YOU TO **ELIMINATE** This man at **0200** hours...

YES, SIR!

This is A **CLASSIFIED OPERATION, SON!**

I WAS THAT **KIND** OF **MARINE** - YOU HAVE A **JOB** TO DO, I'LL **DO IT!**

OCCASIONALLY, THEY WOULD HAVE ME **DRIVE** INTO **DA NANG** TO PICK UP THE **MAIL.**

YOU GO **FAST** AND ANYBODY **IN THE WAY** - YOU **RUN THEM OVER!**

I RAN A BUS OFF THE SIDE OF A MOUNTAIN.

THERE WERE **DEAD CIVILIANS** AT THE BOTTOM IN A **POOL** OF **BLOOD**. THERE WERE **INJURED PEOPLE**...

THE PERSON **WITH** ME WAS VERY **ANGRY** AND **REPORTED ME**. I **LOST** MY **LICENSE**. I JUST THOUGHT I WAS **KILLING COMMIES**!

WHAT'D YA **DO THAT** FOR?

THEY'RE **GOOKS**!

ONE DAY AT THE **BATTERY**, THEY SHOWED ME HOW TO **READ A MAP** & I BECAME A **FORWARD OBSERVER**.

AS AN **F.O.**, IT WAS MY JOB TO **SPOT** THE ENEMY & CALL IN **ARTILLERY** ON THE ENEMY WITHOUT HITTING **OUR OWN GUYS**.

BOOM!

I **WANTED** TO BE **F.O.** I WANTED TO BE THE **HUNTER**, NOT THE **HUNTED**.

I WAS ALMOST **ALWAYS** ATTACHED TO **1ST BATTALION, 1ST MARINES, CHARLIE** COMPANY, AN **INFANTRY** COMPANY NEAR **HOI AN**.

DA NANG

HIEN

QUANG NAM

DA NANG

HOI AN

DIA LOC

DUY XUYEN

T.A.O.R. 1/1 MARINES TOTAL AREA OF RESPONSIBILITY

NAM GIANG

QUE SON

AS AN **ATTACHMENT**, I HAD A **TREMENDOUS** AMOUNT OF **FREEDOM**... NO ONE IN THE IN- FANTRY COULD **FUCK WITH ME**, EXCEPT THE **CAPTAIN** & THE **LIEUTENANT**.

ONCE YOU'RE IN THE **FIELD**, YOU SEE PEOPLE GET **HURT EVERY DAY**... THERE SEEMS TO BE SOMETHING INSIDE YOU THAT WANTS TO **GET EVEN**.

ON **OPERATION STONE**, WE WERE GOING TOWARDS THE VILLAGE, IN **DAI LOC**, AND **SHOOTING** THE PLACE UP.

BEFORE WE WENT OUT ON THE OP- ERATION, WE WERE TOLD WE WERE GOING TO **DESTROY** THE **VILLAGES**, AND WE DIDN'T GIVE THEM ANY **TIME** TO **GET OUT**.

OF COURSE, THEY'RE **RUNNING** TO **GET AWAY**, & BECAUSE THEY'RE **RUNNING**, THAT PROVES THEY'RE **GUILTY**.

AS WE GOT CLOSER TO THE VILLAGE, WE STARTED **BUNCHING UP**.

THERE WAS A **BAMBOO FENCE** AROUND THE **VILLAGE**. THE **LIEUTENANT KICKED OPEN** THE GATE, & A **BOUNCING BETTY MINE** EXPLODED & **GOT** A NUMBER OF US.

WHEN I WOKE UP, I WAS **DISORIENTATED**. I LOOKED AT MY **CROTCH AREA** & I WASN'T **HIT** THERE... I WAS SO **RELIEVED**!

WHEW! They only got my **LEG!** And Now I'm getting a **MEDAL!** I'm gonna get a **PURPLE HEART!**

THAT'S HOW THEY **BUY** YOUR **SOUL**. THEY **PAY** FOR YOUR **SOUL** WITH A **MEDAL**.

MY **RADIO OPERATOR**, HE GOT HIS WHOLE **STOMACH** TORN UP.

I LOST ALL MY **RADIO OPER-ATORS** IN VIETNAM — THEY WERE ALL **WOUNDED**.

HOUSES WERE **BURNED** SO THEY WOULDN'T HAVE **SHELTER**; **CROPS** WERE **BURNED**, **ANIMALS** WERE **KILLED** SO THEY WOULDN'T HAVE **FOOD**...

BODIES WERE DUMPED IN WELLS SO THE WATER COULDN'T BE USED.

TWO PEOPLE HAD THEIR **HEADS CUT OFF** & PUT ON **STAKES**. WE WERE NOTIFIED THAT THERE WAS **PRESS** COVERING THE OPERATION & WE COULDN'T **DO THAT** ANYMORE.

GET those **HEADS** outta Here! The **PRESS** is here with the **VICE PRESIDENT!**

YEAh, the American **PRESS ALWAYS** TELLS The **TRUTH**!

HAW HAW !!!

WE KILLED **EVERYBODY** IN THE **VILLAGE**. (I FOUND OUT LATER) THERE WERE **272** **PEOPLE**.

I WENT **BACK** TO THAT VILLAGE IN **1994** AND THEY HAD A **MEMORIAL** FOR THOSE WHO WERE **KILLED**. I SPENT THE DAY LIGHTING **3 STICKS** OF **INCENSE** FOR EVERY SINGLE GRAVE IN THAT MEMORIAL.

THE **AMAZING** THING IS, ALL THOSE PEOPLE **KNEW** I WAS ONE OF THE GUYS WHO **MURDERED** THOSE PEOPLE - AND THEY WERE ALL **NICE** TO ME!

COULD YOU **IMAGINE SOLDIERS WIPING OUT** A TOWN IN THE U.S., & THEN **COMING BACK** & WANTING TO BE **FRIENDS**?!?!

THE **SOUTH VIETNAMESE**-THEY WERE LIKE A **CANDLE** BEING **BURNED** AT **BOTH ENDS**-THEY DIDN'T STAND A **CHANCE**. THEY WERE REALLY **FUCKED**.

SOMETIMES THEY WOULD **TELL US WHERE** THE **MINES** WERE & WE WOULD **DIG UP** THE MINES...THEN THE **V.C.** WOULD COME IN AND **KILL** EVERYBODY FOR **HELPING US**.

WE OPERATED IN WHAT WE CALLED **"FREE FIRE ZONES."** IT MEANT ANYTHING **LIVE** WAS TO BE **KILLED**.

I WAS TAUGHT THAT THE PEOPLE WHO **STAY** IN A VILLAGE **AFTER** IT'S BEEN **DECLARED** A **FREE FIRE ZONE** WERE THERE TO **PROVIDE SUPPORT** FOR THE **VIET CONG**-THEREFORE, THEY **WERE** THE **VIET CONG**.

THEY GAVE THE **V.C.** FOOD, WATER, INTELLIGENCE & REPAIRED THEM WHEN THEY'RE WOUNDED.

FROM MY POINT OF VIEW, I **DIDN'T KNOW** IF THEY'RE **V.C.** OR IF THEY'RE **GOOD** - IF THEY'RE FUCKING **DEAD** THEY **COULDN'T HURT ME**.

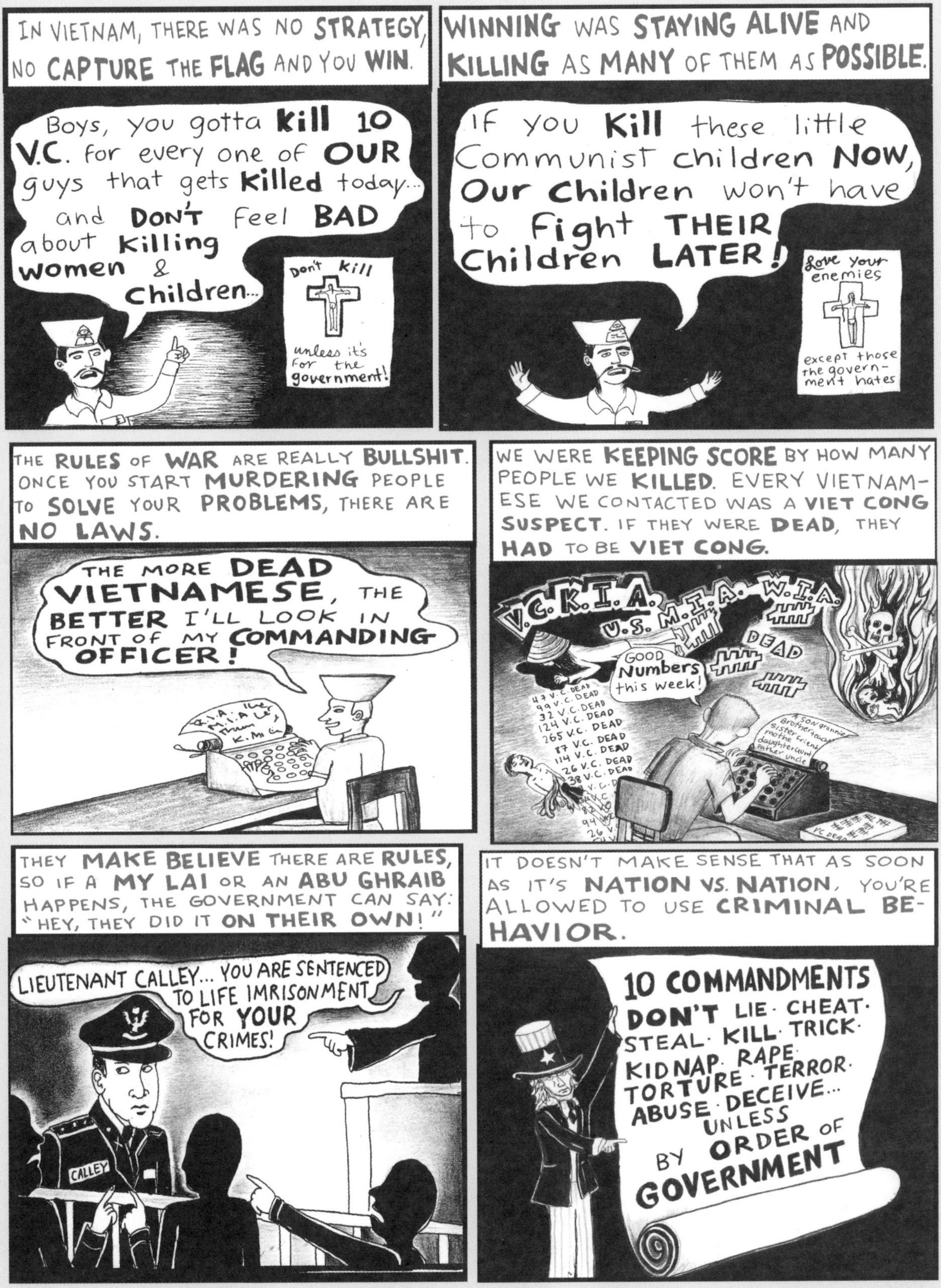
IN VIETNAM, THERE WAS NO STRATEGY, NO CAPTURE THE FLAG AND YOU WIN.
Boys, you gotta Kill 10 V.C. for every one of OUR guys that gets Killed today... and DON'T feel BAD about Killing women & Children...
Don't kill
unless it's for the government!
WINNING WAS STAYING ALIVE AND KILLING AS MANY OF THEM AS POSSIBLE.
If you Kill these little Communist children NOW, Our Children won't have to Fight THEIR Children LATER!
Love your enemies
except those the govern-ment hates
THE RULES OF WAR ARE REALLY BULLSHIT. ONCE YOU START MURDERING PEOPLE TO SOLVE YOUR PROBLEMS, THERE ARE NO LAWS.
THE MORE DEAD VIETNAMESE, THE BETTER I'LL LOOK IN FRONT OF MY COMMANDING OFFICER!
WE WERE KEEPING SCORE BY HOW MANY PEOPLE WE KILLED. EVERY VIETNAMESE WE CONTACTED WAS A VIET CONG SUSPECT. IF THEY WERE DEAD, THEY HAD TO BE VIET CONG.
V.C. K.I.A. U.S. M.I.A. W.I.A.
DEAD
GOOD Numbers this week!
47 V.C. DEAD
99 V.C. DEAD
32 V.C. DEAD
124 V.C. DEAD
265 V.C. DEAD
87 V.C. DEAD
114 V.C. DEAD
26 V.C. DEAD
THEY MAKE BELIEVE THERE ARE RULES, SO IF A MY LAI OR AN ABU GHRAIB HAPPENS, THE GOVERNMENT CAN SAY: "HEY, THEY DID IT ON THEIR OWN!"
LIEUTENANT CALLEY... YOU ARE SENTENCED TO LIFE IMRISONMENT FOR YOUR CRIMES!
CALLEY
IT DOESN'T MAKE SENSE THAT AS SOON AS IT'S NATION VS. NATION, YOU'RE ALLOWED TO USE CRIMINAL BE-HAVIOR.
10 COMMANDMENTS
DON'T LIE · CHEAT · STEAL · KILL · TRICK · KIDNAP · RAPE · TORTURE · TERROR · ABUSE · DECEIVE... UNLESS BY ORDER OF GOVERNMENT

WE WOULD GO THROUGH A VILLAGE AND SAY: "WE DON'T KNOW WHO IT WAS THAT **DID IT**, SO WE WILL **BURN DOWN** THE VILLAGE AND **KILL EVERYBODY!**"

EVERYONE HAD THEIR **OWN LEVEL** OF WHAT THEY WOULD DO. I DIDN'T **TORTURE** MY PRISONERS, BUT I'D **KILL** ANYBODY...

MOST OF THE TIME, I WOULD SAY **70%** OF THE PEOPLE MY UNIT KILLED WERE **WOMEN & CHILDREN**...AND THEY WERE **UNARMED**.

RAPING OF **WOMEN** WAS A **COMMON THING**... WHEN WOMEN WERE **SEARCHED**, THEY WOULD BE **STRIPPED NAKED** & A KIND OF **GAME** WOULD BE MADE OF IT.

Lemme see what you got **HIDDEN** in there!

I NEVER **RAPED** ANYBODY, BUT IF I **SAW** YOU RAPING A WOMAN, I AIN'T GONNA **INTERFERE!**

My **PENIS** IS A **LITTLE LONGER**... I'll use **THAT** instead!

I'M **NEXT!**

ONCE, A WOMAN HAD BEEN **SHOT.** BY THE TIME WE GOT THERE, THE GUYS HAD FINISHED **RAPING** HER & WERE **MUTILATING** HER BODY.

NUO'C! NUO'C! (water)

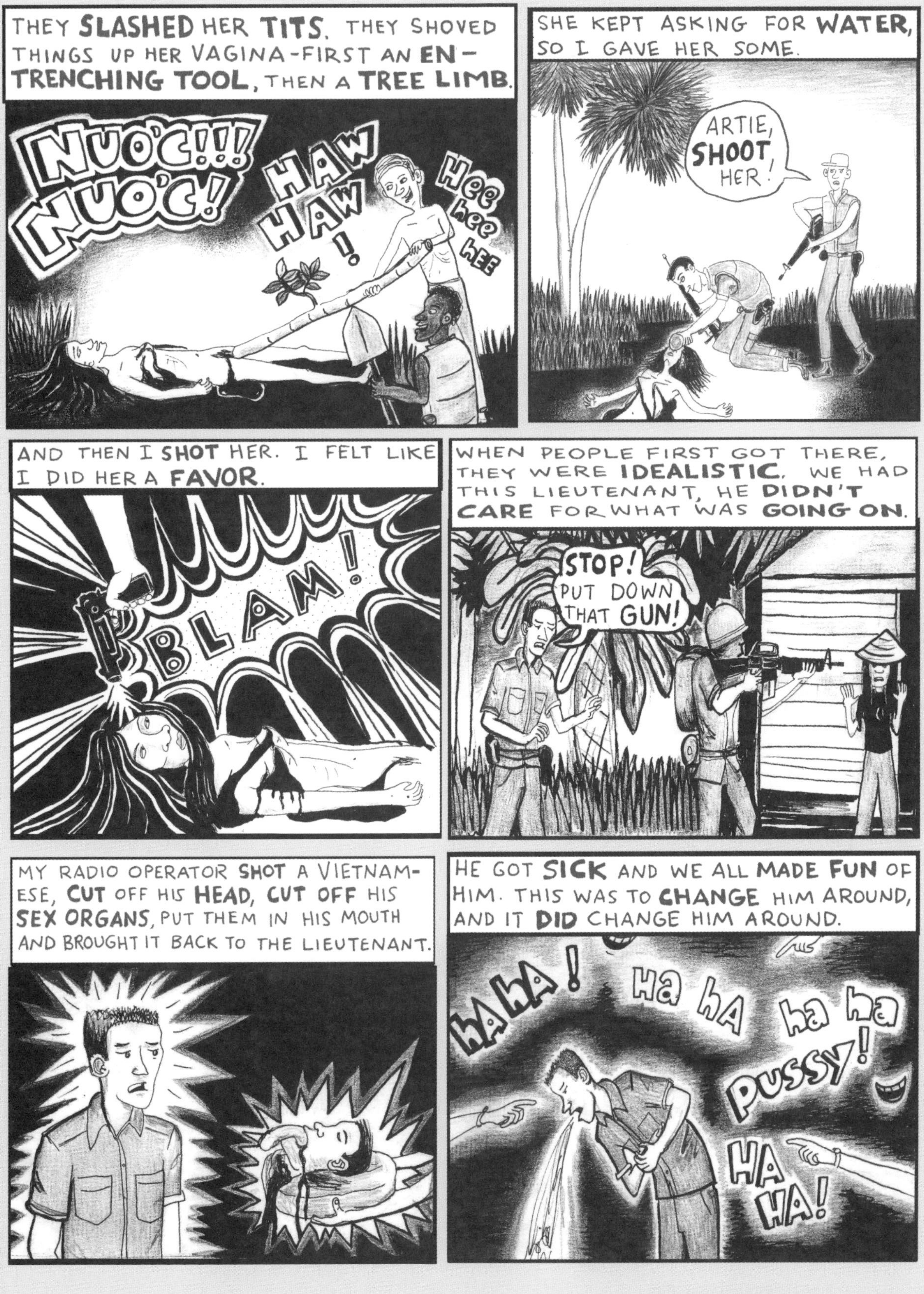

THEY SLASHED HER TITS. THEY SHOVED THINGS UP HER VAGINA-FIRST AN EN-TRENCHING TOOL, THEN A TREE LIMB.
NUO'C!!! NUO'C!
HAW HAW!
Hee hee hee
SHE KEPT ASKING FOR WATER, SO I GAVE HER SOME.
ARTIE, SHOOT HER!
AND THEN I SHOT HER. I FELT LIKE I DID HER A FAVOR.
BLAM!
WHEN PEOPLE FIRST GOT THERE, THEY WERE IDEALISTIC. WE HAD THIS LIEUTENANT, HE DIDN'T CARE FOR WHAT WAS GOING ON.
STOP! PUT DOWN THAT GUN!
MY RADIO OPERATOR SHOT A VIETNAM-ESE, CUT OFF HIS HEAD, CUT OFF HIS SEX ORGANS, PUT THEM IN HIS MOUTH AND BROUGHT IT BACK TO THE LIEUTENANT.
HE GOT SICK AND WE ALL MADE FUN OF HIM. THIS WAS TO CHANGE HIM AROUND, AND IT DID CHANGE HIM AROUND.
HA HA!
Ha hA
ha ha
PUSSY!
HA HA!

THE MORE **RUTHLESS** YOU WERE, THE MORE **RESPECT** YOU GOT. PEOPLE TOOK THEIR **EARS** TO **DA NANG** & TRADED THEM WITH THE **AIR FORCE** FOR **BOOZE**.

I TRIED (CUTTING OFF EARS) ONCE, WITH MY **KA-BAR**, BUT IT WOULDN'T **CUT THROUGH**, SO I STOPPED, AND PEOPLE **LAUGHED** AT ME.

WHEN MY **TOUR** WAS UP, I **EXTENDED** IT FOR ANOTHER **YEAR**.

THERE WAS A **LETTER** I'D WROTE HOME TO MY **MOM** THAT WAS **PUBLISHED** IN MY HOMETOWN NEWSPAPER.

Dear Mom,
I'm **NOT coming back** in **APRIL**, I really **BELIEVE** what we're **DOING** here is **RIGHT** & it's **BETTER** to **STAY** here & get it **CLEARED UP** than for my **BROTHERS** to have to come over **HERE** when they get older!
Love,
Scott

ONE OF THE **PROBLEMS** GUYS HAD **COMING HOME** WAS WHEN THEY LEFT, THINGS **HAPPENED** TO THEIR **BUDDIES** AND THEY **WEREN'T THERE.**

I WAS RAISED TO BELIEVE THAT **REAL MEN** DON'T **LEAVE** THEIR **FRIENDS** IN A **FIGHT**. I DIDN'T WANT TO **LEAVE** MY **BUDDIES**, SO I **STAYED.**

I'VE NEVER BEEN SO **CLOSE** TO OTHER HUMAN BEINGS AS I WAS IN **COMBAT**.

WE REALLY **DEPENDED** ON EACH OTHER.

WE SHARED EACH OTHERS' LETTERS... FOUR OF US SHARED THE SAME TOOTHBRUSH.

IF SOMEONE HAD **SHRAPNEL** IN HIS **ASS**, HE PULLED DOWN HIS PANTS & YOU PUT **MEDICINE** IN HIS ASS.

THEY WOULD CALL YOU **QUEER** IF YOU DID THAT IN **CIVILIAN** LIFE!

I WENT INTO VIETNAM AS A **PRIVATE FIRST CLASS**. AND IN **LESS** THAN **2 YEARS** I WAS A **SERGEANT**. IN COMBAT, **RANK** IS FAST.

I DID BELIEVE WE WERE THERE FOR THE **PROPER REASON**... I DIDN'T RECOGNIZE THAT **REASON** AS BEING **IMPERIALIST** AT THE TIME - I THOUGHT IT WAS MORE HAVING TO DO WITH **FREEDOM**.

IT WAS REALLY **CLEAR** TO ME. I KNEW WHAT **MY JOB** WAS- TO **KILL** THE **VIET CONG**!

I **ENJOYED** IT... I HAD SO MUCH **POWER.** I COULD DECIDE IF YOU WOULD **LIVE** OR **DIE.**

LET'S SEE WHO CAN CALL IN AN **AIR STRIKE** ON that **VILLAGE** FIRST!

LOSER BUYS BEER!

I COULD DECIDE IF YOUR VILLAGE WOULD BE **DESTROYED.**

BLAM!

ANY TIME SOMETHING **CAME UP,** I VOL-**UNTEERED** FOR IT. ON **OPERATION CANYON** I WAS ON A **SCORPION.** WE **HIDE, BLAST 'EM** AND **MELT** IN TO THE **WOODS.**

WE HAD STOPPED TO EAT. ALL OF A SUDDEN, I SAW A WHOLE FUCK-ING **SQUAD** OF **VIET CONG.**

THESE GUYS WERE **MASTERS** OF **CAMOUFLAGE**... TO HAVE A WHOLE **SQUAD** WALK RIGHT IN THE **OPEN,** THAT WAS JUST **WONDERFUL.**

BLAM! BLAM! BLAM!

I KILLED **5** OF THEM. I WAS GIVEN THE **VIETNAMESE CROSS** OF GAL-**LANTRY** WITH THE **SILVER STAR.**

VIETNAMESE CROSS of GALLANTRY with the SILVER STAR

QUAC GIA LAO TRUONG REWARD of the STATE

I DIDN'T FEEL LIKE I WAS IN **DANGER**, SO IT WASN'T REALLY BEING **BRAVE**. I WAS NEVER AFRAID OF GETTING SHOT.

TO ME, **BRAVERY** IS WHEN YOU DO SOMETHING AND YOU DO NOT THINK YOU WILL **SURVIVE** IT.

I WAS SCARED OF **MORTARS** AND STEPPING ON **MINES**... YOU ARE REALLY **HELPLESS**! THAT WOULD GIVE ME **NIGHTMARES**; THAT WOULD **FUCK ME UP**!

ONE TIME, 19 OF US WENT OUT TO A PLACE CALLED "THE **ISLAND**."

WE **KNEW** THAT THE AREA WAS HEAVILY **MINED**. THE LIEUTENANT ASKED THE CAPTAIN **NOT** TO GO OUT.

CAPTAIN, IT'LL BE A **SUICIDE MISSION** TO BRING MY MEN TO THE ISLAND, SIR... I **REQUEST** WE **DON'T GO**.

LIEUTENANT, YOU **HAVE TO GO** AND THAT'S AN **ORDER**!

WE NEVER SAW THE ENEMY AT ALL- IT WAS A **MINEFIELD**. AND THEN THEY **OPENED FIRE** AT US FROM TWO SIDES.

THREE OF US CAME BACK **NOT** DEAD OR WOUNDED... MY FRIEND **DIED** THAT DAY & I WASN'T SURE IF I WAS GOING TO **MAKE IT BACK.**

THE NEXT DAY IN THE **STARS & STRIPES**, THEY SAID WE HAD **KILLED 43** (VIET CONG).

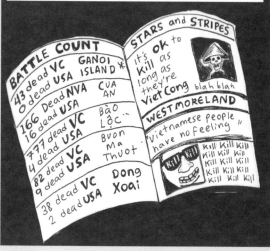

SOON AFTERWARDS, WE MOVED UP TO **QUANG TRI** TO SECURE THE AREA AND BUILD AN AIRSTRIP.

MOST OF THE TIME WE WERE FIGHTING THE **VIET CONG**; NOW WE WERE GOING UP INTO **NORTH VIETNAMESE ARMY** TERRITORY. THE **NVA** WAS NOTED FOR **SUSTAINABLE** FIGHTS — SO WE KNEW THINGS WERE GOING TO BE **HARDER.**

WE WERE GOING TO **SHOW THEM** THAT WE WEREN'T **FUCKING AROUND.** WE GOT DECKS OF CARDS THAT WERE ALL **ACES** OF SPADES.

WE **BURNED** THE VILLAGE DOWN AND **KILLED** EVERYBODY IN IT.

AND THEN WE WENT ON **OPERATION MEDINA** IN A NATIONAL FOREST. IT WAS **TRIPLE CANOPY** JUNGLE.

WE HAVE TO STAY OFF THE TRAILS!

IT WAS A **FIVE BATTALION** OPERATION AND OURS WAS THE **LEAD COMPANY**.

SIR! WE HAVE TO **STAY OFF** THE **TRAILS**! TRAILS AND ROADS LEAD TO **AMBUSHES**! IT'LL TAKE **LONGER**, BUT WE'LL GO THROUGH THE **BRUSH**!

YOU'RE **NOT** MEETING YOUR **OBJECTIVES**! GET **ON** THAT **TRAIL** AND THAT'S AN **ORDER**!

WHEN WE WALKED (ON THE TRAIL), THEY WERE IN THE **TREES**, DROPPING **GRENADES** ON US.

BOOM!

AND THEY JUST **WIPED** THE **SHIT** OUT OF **EVERYBODY**.

WE WERE REALLY GETTING OUR ASSES KICKED!

MOMMY!

AAARRGGHH!

CORPSMAN!

I THINK THEY HAD A **VENDETTA** TO **GET BACK AT US** FOR WHAT WE DID TO THAT **VILLAGE**.

THAT DAY, I WAS THINKING I WAS **GONNA DIE**. I WAS **OUT** OF **AMMO** AND **MAD** AT MYSELF FOR **STAYING** AN **EXTRA TOUR** WHEN I COULD'VE **GONE HOME**.

I GOT **WOUNDED** BY A **GRENADE**.

ALL AROUND ME WERE **DEAD PEOPLE**. I CRAWLED OVER TO THEM TO GET THEIR **AMMO** & WATER & MEDICAL SUPPLIES.

THAT WAS THE ONLY TIME IN MY LIFE THAT I **CONTEMPLATED SUICIDE**.

IN MY **HEART**, I WANTED TO **LIVE**.

BUT WE WERE RESCUED!

AFTER THAT BATTLE, WE WERE ALL **OLD MEN.**

THE **NEWSPAPERS** SAID WE HAD ALL THESE **KILLS**... I DIDN'T SEE IT... THEY JUST DIDN'T WANT TO **ADMIT** THAT ALL THOSE GUYS **DIED** FOR **NOTHING!**

THEN, I'M **BACK** TO THE UNIT FOR TWO WEEKS. I WAS WOUNDED & SHOOK UP BUT I STILL FELT IT WAS COWARDICE TO LEAVE...

IN REALITY, I WAS AFRAID TO ADMIT THAT I WAS **SCARED** AND I WANTED TO **GO HOME.**

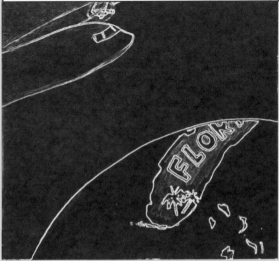

MY FIRST SERGEANT COULD SEE I WAS REALLY **SHOT.**

I HAD **TWO YEARS** LEFT IN THE **MARINE CORPS**... AND THAT HELPED ME IMMENSELY. IF I HAD GONE **STRAIGHT** FROM **VIETNAM** TO THE **STREETS**, I WOULD'VE BEEN **WILD**.

CAMP LEJEUNE, NORTH CAROLINA

ONE DAY YOU ARE **KILLING PEOPLE**, THE **NEXT DAY** YOU ARE WALKING AROUND **HOME** AND THE FUCKING **COPS** ARE PUSHING YOU AROUND.

THURSDAY   FRIDAY

You **COME BACK** TO THE **STATES** AND YOU **AIN'T SHIT**. NOBODY GIVES A **SHIT** ABOUT YOUR **SACRIFICES**.

DRAFT DEFERMENT 4-F

Bread & Circus

WE ARE SUPPOSED TO **FALL** IN **LINE** AND BE **REGULAR DUDES** AGAIN BUT YOU CAN'T TAKE THOSE EXPERIENCES **OUT** OF A PERSON.

MEDICINE 3rd LEADING CAUSE OF DEATH SINCE

NOW, TAKE these **PILLS** and **SHUT UP!**

What's **IN** them?

DON'T ASK DON'T TELL.

V.A. HOSPITAL
PAULREUTERSHAMWING

I WAS IN **CAMP LEJEUNE**, BUT EVERY TIME A **QUOTA** CAME UP FOR A **SCHOOL**, I WENT.

PS Y OPS SCHOOL

RIOT CONTROL

REVOLUTION

YAY! YAY!

EMBARCATION SCHOOL

US NAVY

NUCLEAR CHEMICAL BIOLOGICAL WEAPONS TRAINING

I WAS SENT TO **NUCLEAR, BIOLOGICAL** AND **CHEMICAL** WARFARE SCHOOL AT **CAMP GEIGER**.

EMPIRE

USA INCORPORATED IN DELAWARE

APPROX. 7-800 U.S. BASES AROUND THE WORLD.

DUN + BRADSTREET

REPORT TO CAMP GEIGER NUCLEAR BIOLOGICAL CHEMICAL WEAPONS TRAINING

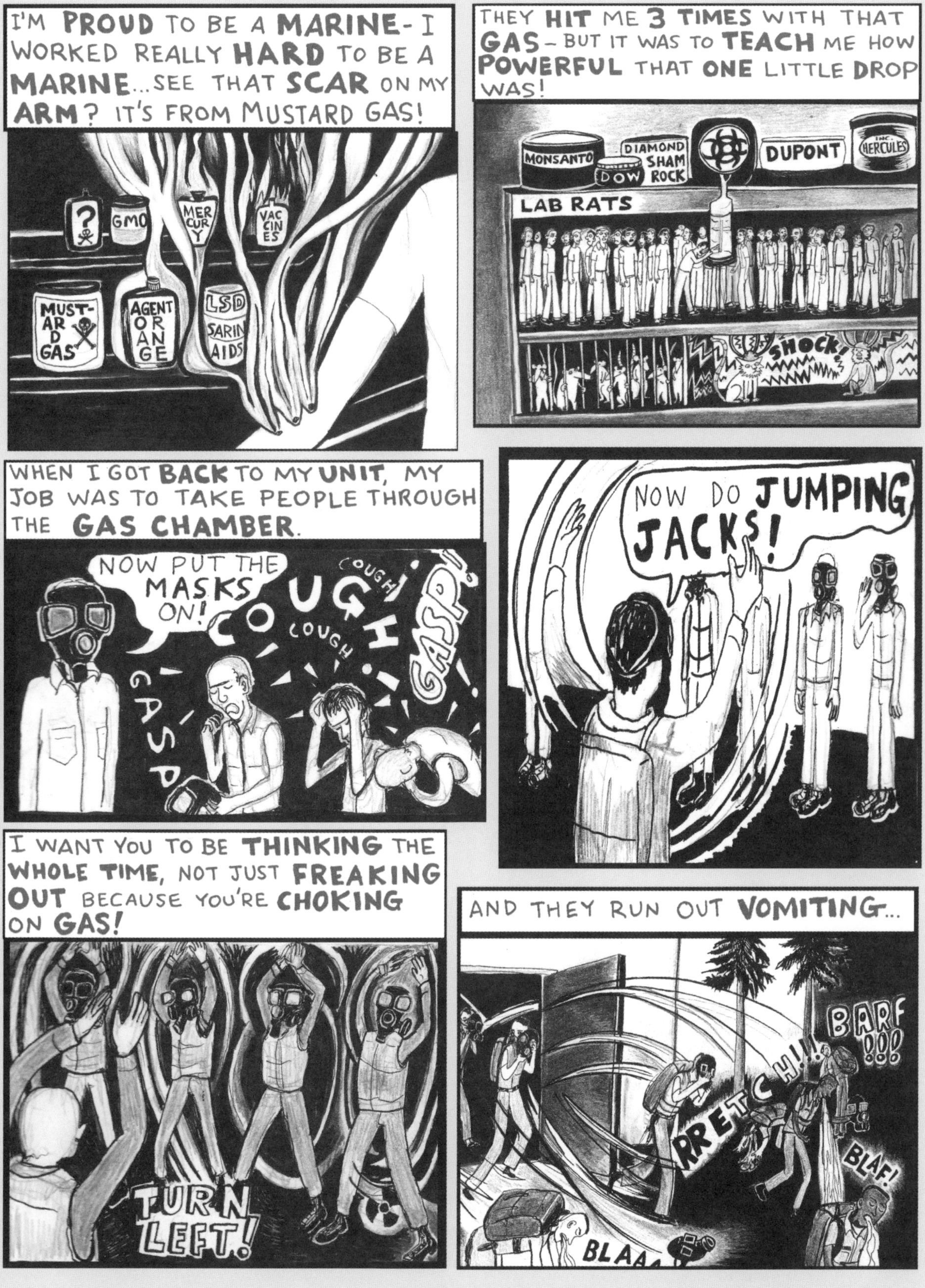

I'M PROUD TO BE A MARINE- I WORKED REALLY HARD TO BE A MARINE...SEE THAT SCAR ON MY ARM? IT'S FROM MUSTARD GAS!
?
GMO
MER CURY
VAC CIN ES
MUST-AR D GAS
AGENT OR AN GE
LSD
SARIN
AIDS
THEY HIT ME 3 TIMES WITH THAT GAS - BUT IT WAS TO TEACH ME HOW POWERFUL THAT ONE LITTLE DROP WAS!
MONSANTO
DOW
DIAMOND SHAM ROCK
DUPONT
INC. HERCULES
LAB RATS
SHOCK!
WHEN I GOT BACK TO MY UNIT, MY JOB WAS TO TAKE PEOPLE THROUGH THE GAS CHAMBER.
NOW PUT THE MASKS ON!
COUGH
COUGH
COUGH
GASP!
GASP
NOW DO JUMPING JACKS!
I WANT YOU TO BE THINKING THE WHOLE TIME, NOT JUST FREAKING OUT BECAUSE YOU'RE CHOKING ON GAS!
TURN LEFT!
AND THEY RUN OUT VOMITING...
BARF!!!
RRETCH!!!
BLAF!
BLAA

THEY SENT ME TO **EMBARKATION SCHOOL** FOR SIX WEEKS TO LEARN HOW TO **LOAD SHIPS**...

AND WE SPENT **6 MONTHS** ON A SHIP TO **EUROPE**.

US FT MANDAN LSD 21

I GOT SO **SEASICK** ON THIS TRIP, I ASKED MY **COMMANDING OFFICER** TO SEND ME **BACK** TO **VIETNAM**!

SEND ME **BACK** TO **VIETNAM**!

We'll **FLY** you back to **VIETNAM**, but then you'll have to **sign up** for **6** more **YEARS!**

SO I GOT A **KILO** OF **STICKY** POT IN **BARCELONA** AND A **KILO** OF **HASH** FROM **TURKEY**.

SUDDENLY, **NONE** OF THE **MARINES** WERE **SICK** ANYMORE...

WELL, THEY FLEW OUT IN **HELI-COPTERS** & **RAIDED** THE **SHIP!**

THEY SEARCHED **EVERY BAG** BUT THEY DIDN'T FIND **MY STUFF!**

THE **NAVY GUYS** ALL ADMITTED TO **SMOKING POT** & GOT IN **TROUBLE;** THE MARINES **DENIED** IT!

NONE OF THE NAVY GUYS WOULD **TESTIFY AGAINST** US, 'CAUSE THEY THOUGHT WE WOULD **KILL** THEM — & **MAYBE** WE **WOULD HAVE!**

YOU CAN BE **ALIVE** ONE MINUTE AND **DEAD** THE NEXT — SO I WANTED TO **LIVE** FOR **NOW**, I WANTED TO HAVE **FUN!**

TO ME, **FUN** WAS **SEX & DRUGS.** EVERY WEEKEND, I'D DRIVE TO MY **GIRLFRIEND'S** AND **STAY OUT** UNTIL **MONDAY** FORMATION.

ONE OF THE **SCHOOLS** THEY SENT ME TO WAS **RIOT CONTROL**. I BECAME THE **RIOT CONTROL N.C.O.**

SO BASICALLY AT THE **SCHOOL**, THEY TEACH US THAT WE'RE **NOT** THE **JUDGE** OR **JURY**.

WHEN I WAS IN **VIETNAM**, I READ AN ARTICLE ABOUT **JOAN BAEZ** AND HER **FRIENDS**...

I CAN'T TELL YOU HOW **ANGRY** THAT MADE ME THAT I COULD GET **KILLED** BY SOME FUCKING **COMMIE** WITH **AMERICAN BLOOD** IN HIS **VEINS!**

SO NOW IT'S A **THURSDAY** & THE **FIRST SERGEANT** SAYS WE'RE ON **STANDBY**. NOW I CAN'T GO **HOME** AND GET **LAID!**

SO THE **ANTI-WAR** PEOPLE WERE **REALLY** ON MY **SHIT LIST!!**

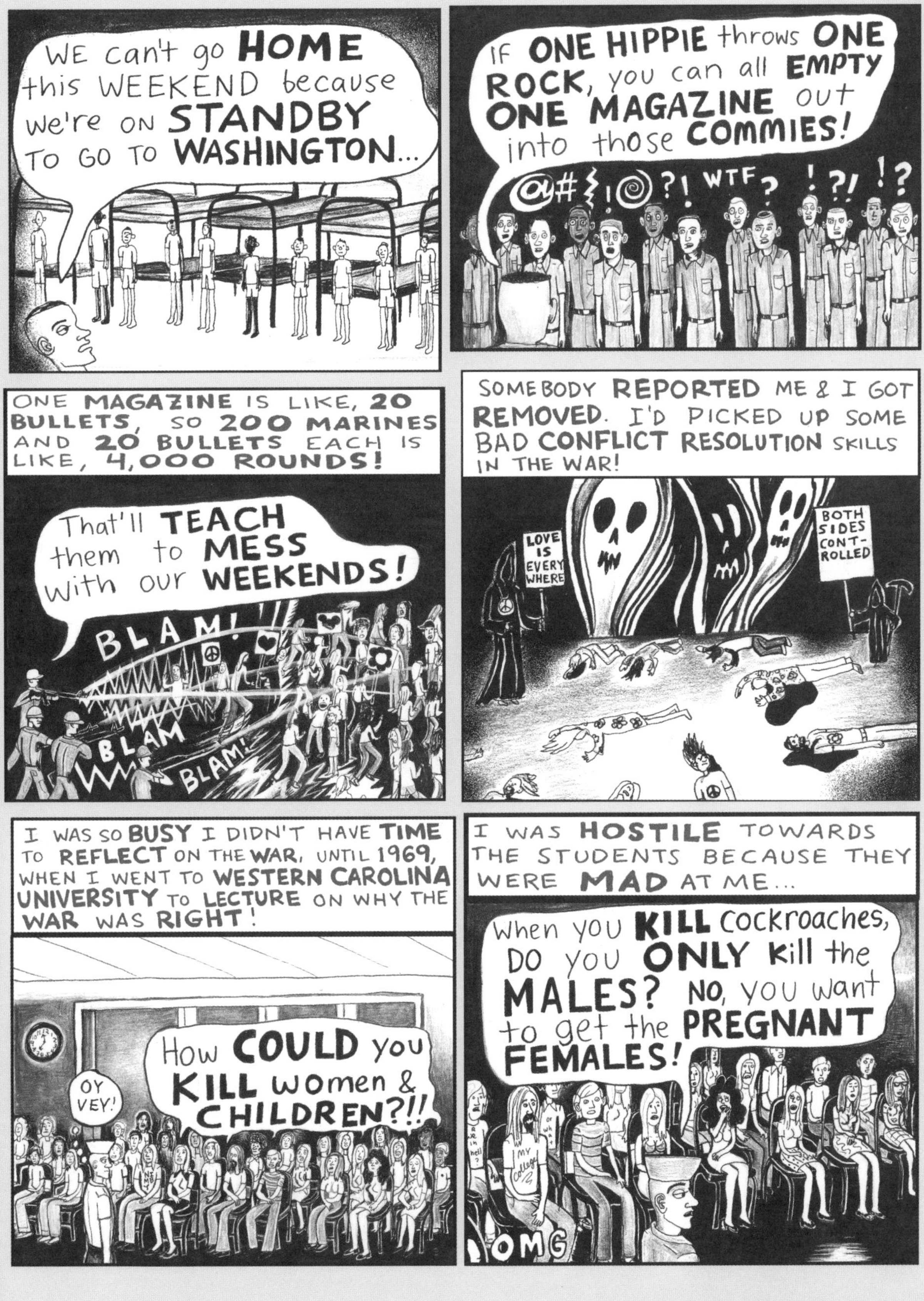

WE can't go HOME this WEEKEND because we're ON STANDBY TO GO TO WASHINGTON...
IF ONE HIPPIE throws ONE ROCK, you can all EMPTY ONE MAGAZINE out into those COMMIES!
?! WTF ? ! ?! !?
ONE MAGAZINE IS LIKE, 20 BULLETS, SO 200 MARINES AND 20 BULLETS EACH IS LIKE, 4,000 ROUNDS!
That'll TEACH them to MESS with our WEEKENDS!
BLAM!
BLAM
BLAM!
SOMEBODY REPORTED ME & I GOT REMOVED. I'D PICKED UP SOME BAD CONFLICT RESOLUTION SKILLS IN THE WAR!
LOVE IS EVERY WHERE
BOTH SIDES CONT-ROLLED
I WAS SO BUSY I DIDN'T HAVE TIME TO REFLECT ON THE WAR, UNTIL 1969, WHEN I WENT TO WESTERN CAROLINA UNIVERSITY TO LECTURE ON WHY THE WAR WAS RIGHT!
OY VEY!
How COULD you KILL women & CHILDREN?!!
I WAS HOSTILE TOWARDS THE STUDENTS BECAUSE THEY WERE MAD AT ME...
When you KILL cockroaches, DO you ONLY kill the MALES? NO, you want to get the PREGNANT FEMALES!
MY college
OMG

I WAS STILL IN THE **MARINES** AND **PROUD** OF **SERVING** MY **COUNTRY**...

THAT WAS THE **FIRST** TIME I GOT IN **TROUBLE** FOR TELLING THE **TRUTH** ABOUT **VIETNAM**.

I WASN'T PLANNING ON **STAYING** IN THE **MARINES**. I HAVE A STRONG **ANTI-AUTHORITY** STREAK. I DON'T LIKE **STUPID** PEOPLE TELLING ME **WHAT** TO DO.

I LEARNED IN **VIETNAM** THAT THE PEOPLE WHO WERE IN **CHARGE**, WHO WERE SUPPOSED TO **KNOW** EVERYTHING, **DIDN'T KNOW SHIT!**

WHEN I **GOT OUT** OF THE MILITARY, I HADN'T THE **SLIGHTEST IDEA** WHAT I'D **DO**.

MY **STEPFATHER** WAS A **COP**, MY **2 BROTHERS** WERE **COPS**, SO I APPLIED TO BE A **MIAMI COP**.

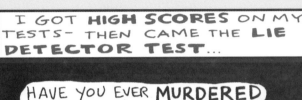

I WAS **DEVASTATED**. I DIDN'T THINK I WAS DOING ANYTHING **WRONG**.

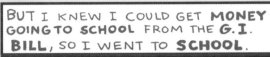

YOU **SMOKED MARIJUANA!??** YOU **KNOWINGLY VIOLATED** the **LAW!** you have **NO RESPECT** for the **LAW!**

I (WENT) DOWN TO THE FEDERAL BUILD-ING TO INQUIRE ABOUT BEING A **SKY MARSHAL**...

BUT I KNEW I COULD GET **MONEY GOING TO SCHOOL** FROM THE **G.I. BILL**, SO I WENT TO **SCHOOL**.

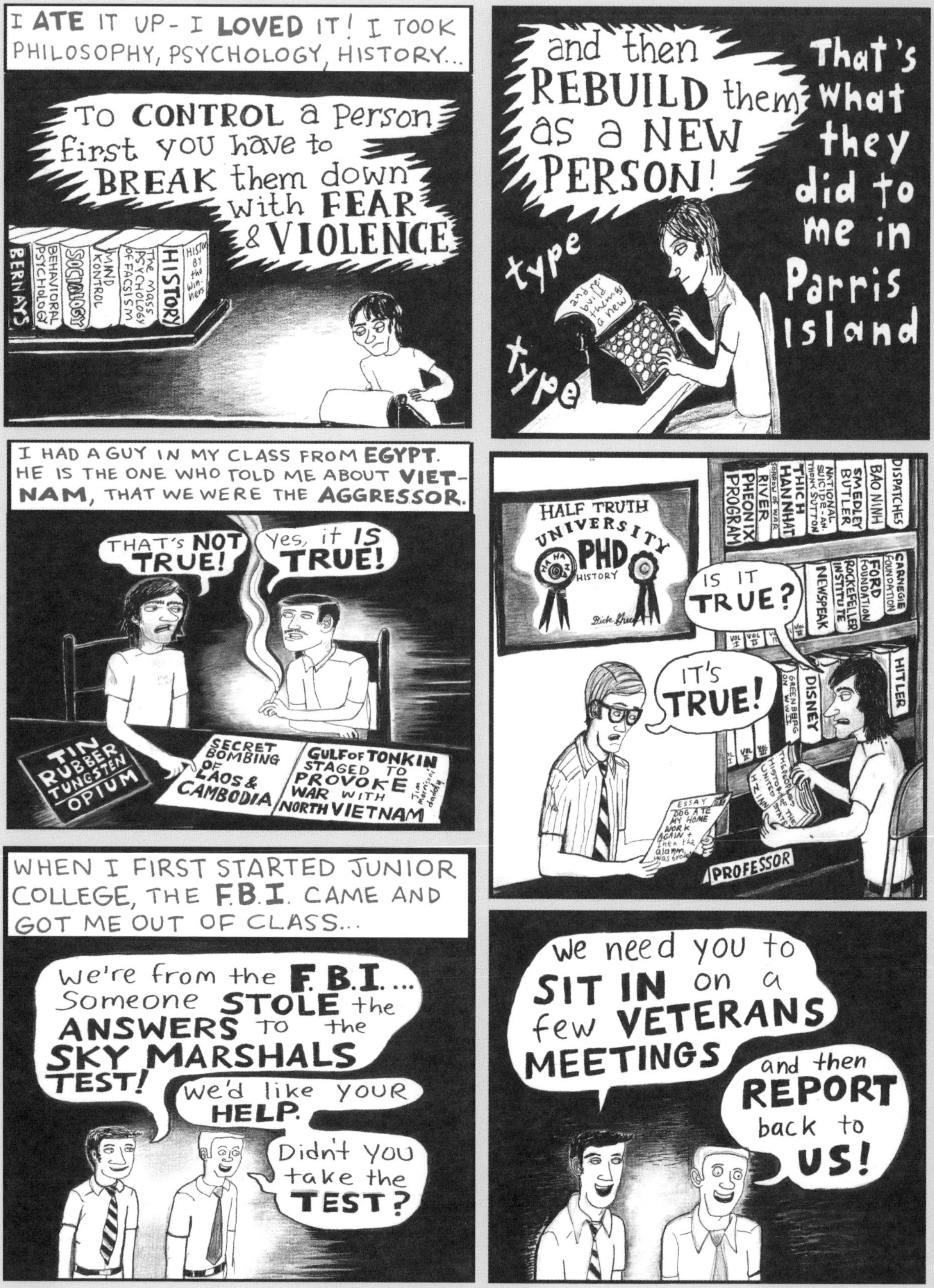
I ATE IT UP - I LOVED IT! I TOOK PHILOSOPHY, PSYCHOLOGY, HISTORY...
TO CONTROL a person first you have to BREAK them down with FEAR & VIOLENCE
BERNAYS
BEHAVIORAL PSYCHOLOGY
SOCIOLOGY
MIND KONTROL
THE MASS PSYCHOLOGY OF FACSISM
HISTORY
and then REBUILD them as a NEW PERSON!
That's what they did to me in Parris Island
type
type
I HAD A GUY IN MY CLASS FROM EGYPT. HE IS THE ONE WHO TOLD ME ABOUT VIET-NAM, THAT WE WERE THE AGGRESSOR.
THAT'S NOT TRUE!
Yes, it IS TRUE!
TIN RUBBER TUNGSTEN OPIUM
SECRET BOMBING OF LAOS & CAMBODIA
GULF OF TONKIN STAGED TO PROVOKE WAR WITH NORTH VIETNAM
HALF TRUTH UNIVERSITY PHD HISTORY
PHEONIX PROGRAM
RIVER
THICH HANNHAT
NATIONAL SUICIDE
SMEDLEY BUTLER
BAO NINH
DISPATCHES
NEWSPEAK
ROCKEFELLER INSTITUTE
FORD FOUNDATION
CARNEGIE FOUNDATION
IS IT TRUE?
IT'S TRUE!
DISNEY
HITLER
PROFESSOR
WHEN I FIRST STARTED JUNIOR COLLEGE, THE F.B.I. CAME AND GOT ME OUT OF CLASS...
We're from the F.B.I.... Someone STOLE the ANSWERS to the SKY MARSHALS TEST!
We'd like YOUR HELP.
Didn't you take the TEST?
We need you to SIT IN on a few VETERANS MEETINGS
and then REPORT back to US!

THE BOTTOM LINE WAS, IT DID **NOT** WORK OUT!

WHY would I want to **SPY** on people? why do you **BUST** people for smoking **WEED**?

Thank you for your **TIME**, Mr. **CAMIL**.

I TRANSFERED UP (TO **UNIVERSITY** OF **FLORIDA** AT **GAINESVILLE**) IN **JANUARY** OF 1971.

WHEN I FIRST GOT HERE, I HEARD THAT BLACK STUDENTS HAD BEEN **ARRESTED** FOR **DEMONSTRATING** AND SOME TEACHERS HAD BEEN **FIRED** FOR **ANTI-WAR** ACTIVITIES.

ONE HUMAN RACE

WAR IS GENOCIDE

WAR IS TERRORISM

BLACK IS BEAUTIFUL

EXIT

UF GO GATORS

AT **MIAMI-DADE**, THE **ANTI-WAR** PEOPLE WOULD WEAR **BLACK ARM-BANDS** AND THEY WOULD **BOYCOTT**.

Fucking **HIPPIES!**

HONEYWELL LOCKHEED MARTIN INGERSOL RAND RAYTHEON

USA

BROWN & ROOT BECHTEL MONSANTO

BOYCOTT WAR PROFITEERS

NORTHROP GRUBMAN

DUPONT

WE WANTA **PEACE ECONOMY**

I WOULD **BUMP INTO** THEM AND **PICK FIGHTS** WITH THEM.

HEY COMMIE! OUTTA MY WAY

!!

Traitor!

STOP THE WAR

I **HATED** THESE **MUTHERFUCKERS**, THESE **COMMIE SYMPATHIZERS**, EVEN **AFTER** MY PROFESSOR TOLD ME THE **STUFF** IN THE **BOOK** ABOUT **VIETNAM** WAS **TRUE!**

We're dirty hippie Commies we hate AMERICA and the FLAG!

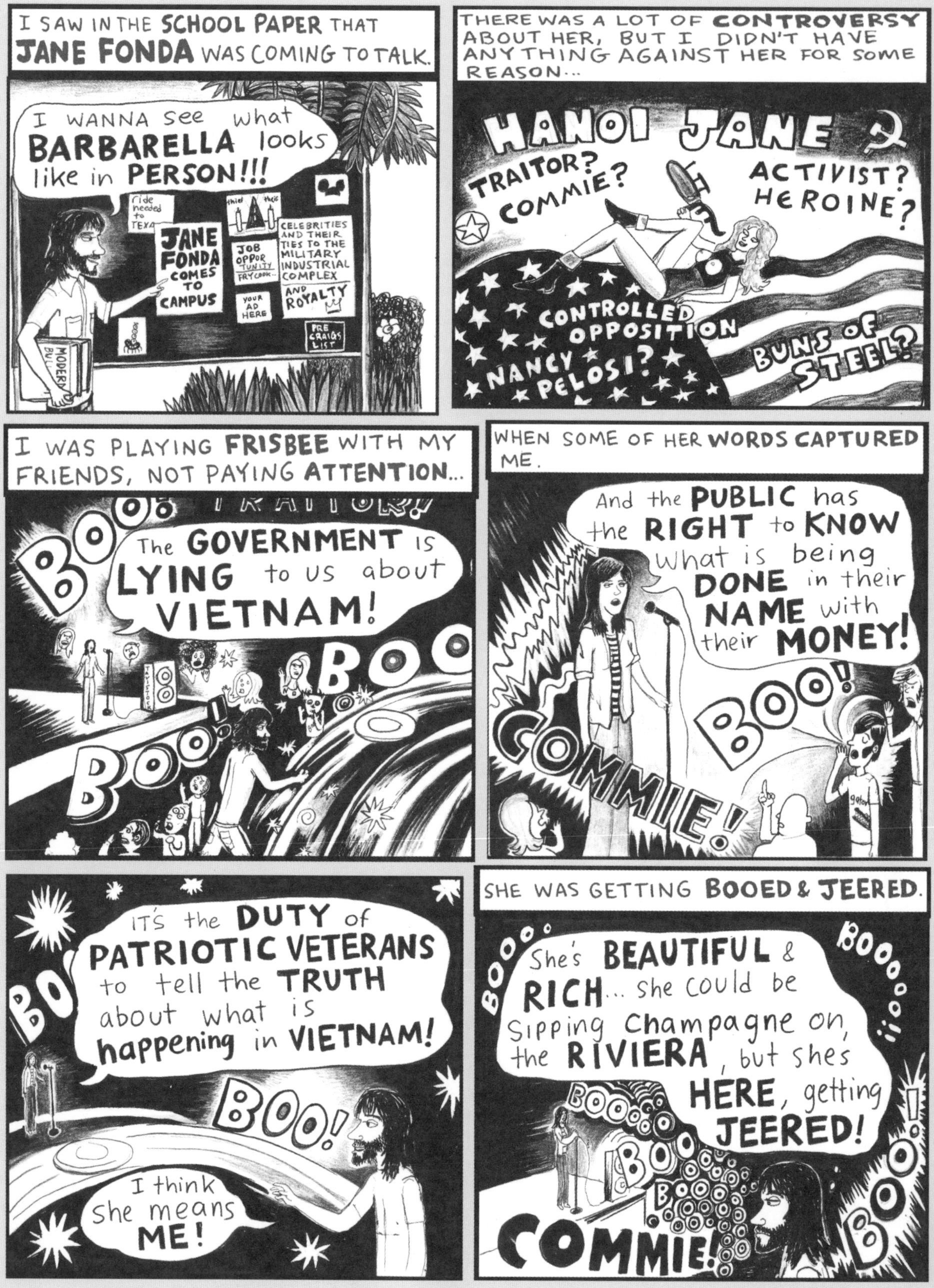
I SAW IN THE SCHOOL PAPER THAT JANE FONDA WAS COMING TO TALK.
I WANNA see what BARBARELLA looks like in PERSON!!!
JANE FONDA COMES TO CAMPUS
JOB OPPORTUNITY FRY COOK...
CELEBRITIES AND THEIR TIES TO THE MILITARY INDUSTRIAL COMPLEX AND ROYALTY
YOUR AD HERE
PRE CRAIGS LIST
THERE WAS A LOT OF CONTROVERSY ABOUT HER, BUT I DIDN'T HAVE ANYTHING AGAINST HER FOR SOME REASON...
HANOI JANE
TRAITOR? COMMIE?
ACTIVIST? HEROINE?
CONTROLLED OPPOSITION
NANCY PELOSI?
BUNS OF STEEL?
I WAS PLAYING FRISBEE WITH MY FRIENDS, NOT PAYING ATTENTION...
BOO! TRAITOR!
The GOVERNMENT is LYING to us about VIETNAM!
BOO
BOO!
WHEN SOME OF HER WORDS CAPTURED ME.
And the PUBLIC has the RIGHT to KNOW what is being DONE in their NAME with their MONEY!
BOO!
COMMIE!
IT'S the DUTY of PATRIOTIC VETERANS to tell the TRUTH about what is happening in VIETNAM!
BOO!
I think she means ME!
SHE WAS GETTING BOOED & JEERED.
She's BEAUTIFUL & RICH... she could be sipping champagne on, the RIVIERA, but shes HERE, getting JEERED!
BOOOO
BOOOO!
COMMIE!

I AGREED THAT THE **PUBLIC** OUGHT TO **KNOW** THE **TRUTH**...

SO I WENT FORWARD TO **MEET** WITH THEM.

I WAS **LOOKING** FOR **RECOGNITION**. I WANTED TO **BRAG** ABOUT ALL THE **GOOKS** I HAD **KILLED**. I WANTED TO **SHOW OFF** MY **MEDALS**.

I WAS **PROUD** OF WHAT I **DID** AND WAS **LOOKING** FOR SOME FUCKING **THANKS**!

SOMEONE **PAID** FOR MY **PLANE TICKET** & FLEW ME UP TO **DETROIT** WITH MY DOCUMENTATION.

FOR 3 DAYS, I LISTENED TO ALL THESE PEOPLE **TESTIFYING**...

I MET SOME **VIETNAMESE** THERE, AND THEY WERE **NICE** PEOPLE; I FINALLY RECOGNIZED THAT THEY WERE **HUMAN BEINGS**.

THINGS WERE STARTING TO COME TOGETHER...

WHEN YOU **FIRST** GET TO **VIETNAM**, YOU'RE SO **SCARED** YOU MAKE THE **ENEMY** INTO AN **ANIMAL** & YOU TURN **YOURSELF** INTO AN **ANIMAL**!

NOW, I WAS STARTING TO THINK THAT **WE** WERE THE **BAD GUYS**.

I HAD TO **ADMIT** THAT I WAS A **MURDERER**... THAT I HAD MURDERED PEOPLE WHO WERE **DEFENDING** THEIR **HOMES**.

WE WERE **SOLDIERS ALL** THE **WAY**! THE **INDOCTRINATION** & TRAINING MAKE YOU THAT WAY! THEY **DEHUMANIZE** YOU SO MUCH, THE **ENEMY** IS NO LONGER A **MAN** - IT'S A **TARGET**!

I GREW UP AS A **JEWISH PERSON** & WAS TOLD THE STORIES OF MY **FAMILY** WHO WERE **KILLED** IN **CONCENTRATION CAMPS**... NOW I FIND OUT THAT **I** WAS THE **FUCKING NAZI**!

I KEPT TRYING TO **JUSTIFY** IT, BUT I **KNEW** IT **WASN'T RIGHT**... I HAD TO **ADMIT** WHAT I DID WAS **WRONG** & TRY TO **STOP** OTHER PEOPLE FROM **MAKING** THE **SAME MISTAKE** I MADE!

IT'S REALLY **HARD**, WHEN YOU HAVE **FAITH** IN THINGS LIKE A **SOCIETY**, TO **LOSE** THAT **FAITH**.

the whole thing (in Boot Camp), is about **CONTROLLING** YOUR **MIND** AND IF THEY can **GET** TO YOUR **MIND**, THEY can get YOU TO **DO ANYTHING**!

the milgram experiments

THE **BLOOD** THAT I **SPILLED** ON THE **GROUND** IN **VIETNAM** WAS **WASTED**.

WE DID TO THE **VIETNAMESE** SAME AS THEY DID TO THE **INDIANS**!

NOWADAYS, THEY USE **CHEMICAL WARFARE** ...BACK THEN, THEY'D PUT **SMALL POX** ON A **BLANKET**...

MY **BUDDIES** HAD **DIED** FOR **NOTHING**.

SINCE I WAS **SMALL** I WAS **EXPOSED** (TO THIS CULTURE)... WHEN I WATCHED **TV** AND IT WAS **CAVALRY** AGAINST THE **INDIANS**... I'D **CHEER** FOR THE **CAVALRY**! THAT'S HOW **BAD** IT WAS!

WE WERE **USED** & **LIED** TO BY OUR **GOVERNMENT** & ALL OUR **SACRIFICES** WERE FOR **NOTHING**!

ON THE **LAST DAY**, A GUY NAMED **MIKE OLIVER** HAD A **MEETING** WITH ALL THE **VETERANS**...

They're still **KILLING** people over there who are just **PROTECTING** THEIR **HOMES** IT'S TRUE!

FREE PELTIER

ALREADY, THERE WAS A **VIETNAM VETERANS AGAINST** THE **WAR** IN NEW JERSEY, PENNSYLVANIA & NEW YORK...

IT'S **OUR JOB** TO **STOP** THE **KILLING**! **AIN'T NOBODY ELSE** GONNA **DO** IT.

He's **right**!

& NOW THEY WERE GOING **NATIONWIDE**.

WE NEED TO **ORGANIZE**! WE NEED ONE OF THESE **DISPLAYS** IN **EVERY TOWN** ACROSS THE **COUNTRY**!

I'M GONNA **DO THIS**.... I'M GONNA BE **PART** OF THIS!

I'M GONNA START A **WINTER SOLDIER** IN GAINESVILLE!

THE **ORGANIZERS** HAD ORGANIZED **UNIONS** & **CIVIL RIGHTS** STUFF.

don't get MAD, ORGANIZE!!!

PEACEFUL NON COMPLIANCE

BOYCOTT

TRUTH

STRIKE

UNION MADE IN AMERICA

PUSH BACK

THE **ANTI-WAR PEOPLE**, THEY WERE MY FUCKING **ENEMIES**... AND NOW I GO TO **WINTER SOLDIER** – ALL OF A SUDDEN, I'M ONE OF **THEM!**

I CAME BACK TO GAINESVILLE & BACK TO **VETS FOR PEACE** TO GIVE THEM A REPORT. THEY WERE REAL **COLD** TO ME...

WE should have a **WINTER SOLDIER** here in **GAINESVILLE!**

Who **ARE** you?

You could be a **COP** for all we know!

Why would a **COP** want to be in an **ANTI-WAR** GROUP?!?

ha ha! You're **NEW** to this!

WORLD PIECE

Vets for

AT THE END OF FEBRUARY, I GOT A CALL TO GO TO **NEW YORK** & HELP SET UP **V.V.A.W. NATIONALLY.**

Scott, we'll **FLY** you to **NEW YORK**... WE WANT YOU TO **REPRESENT** the **SOUTH!**

WE DREW UP THE **CONSTITUTION**; WE **FOUGHT** OVER EVERY FUCKING WORD!

BOYCOTTS!

WE'LL **MARCH** ON **WASHINGTON** And

PROTESTS!

THROW AWAY

MEDALS ON THE WHITE HOUSE LAWN!

ALL THESE PEOPLE ARE **NOT TO-GETHER** ON **ANYTHING** EXCEPT WE ALL THINK THE **WAR** IS **WRONG.**

The **PROBLEM** IS **CLASS!**

NO, it's **REPUB-LICAN!**

NO it's!

NO, IT'S **RACE!**

NO, **DEMOCRATS!**

CAN WE JUST **FOCUS** ON **STOPPING** The **WAR!**

WE WERE PLANNING A **MARCH** ON **WASHINGTON** TO THROW OUR **MEDALS** AWAY.

I HAVE TO TELL YOU, I WAS ONE OF THE **RADICALS** — MY PLAN WAS TO JUST **SHOOT** THE BASTARDS!

JUST THE FACT THAT IT WAS **DISCUSSED PISSED** SOME PEOPLE OFF. IT WAS THE MOST **DIVISIVE** THING THAT TOOK PLACE.

THERE WERE PEOPLE WHO ACCUSED ME OF BEING AN **UNDERCOVER AGENT** — I WAS SO **NAIVE**, I DIDN'T **KNOW** ANYTHING ABOUT **AGENTS**.

I BELIEVED **FREE SPEECH** MEANT I COULD **SAY** WHATEVER I **WANTED**.

THERE WAS A **VOTE** & IT WAS **VOTED DOWN.**

When you **KILL** a **SNAKE,** do you **CUT OFF** its **HEAD** or its **TAIL?**

He's a **COP!**

HAD WE **DONE** IT, I DON'T BELIEVE WE'D BE IN **IRAQ** OR **AFGHANISTAN** NOW— WE WOULDN'T HAVE **NONE** OF THIS **SHIT!**

TOP SECRET ILLUMINATI COUNCIL

NEW WORLD ORDER

If they keep **KILLING** our **PUPPETS** in office, No one's going to want to **SPONSOR** our blood **SACRIFICES...** um, **wars...**

SO, I STARTED MY OWN GROUP, THE **GAINESVILLE** CHAPTER OF THE **V.V.A.W.** (VIETNAM VETERANS AGAINST THE WAR).

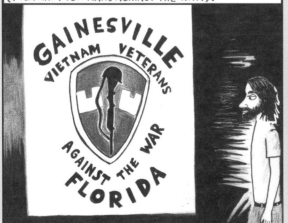

GAINESVILLE VIETNAM VETERANS AGAINST THE WAR FLORIDA

THESE GUYS (IN CONGRESS) WERE JUST AS **ARROGANT** THEN AS THEY ARE TODAY. THESE **ASSHOLES** GAVE THEMSELVES **PAY RAISES** IN THE MIDDLE OF THE NIGHT FOR **MISMANAGING** THE **COUNTRY.**

K STREET FUNDRAISER

VOTE FOR ME

WE DIVIDED THE COUNTRY INTO **28 SECTORS** – I BECAME THE COORDINATOR FOR THE **SOUTHEASTERN** UNITED STATES.

KY TENN NC ALA GA SC MISS

THAT FEBRUARY, **PLAYBOY** GAVE **V.V.A.W.** A **FREE, FULL-PAGE AD** INVITING PEOPLE TO **JOIN,** & THAT GENERATED SOMETHING LIKE **20,000 RESPONSES.**

339,000 HAVE been killed or wounded in Vietnam, more are being killed or wounded every day. We don't think it's **WORTH IT.**

I STARTED TRAVELING AROUND TO ALL THESE CITIES, SETTING UP **WINTER SOLDIER INVESTIGATIONS** ALL OVER THE **SOUTHEAST.**

WE HAD **WINTER SOLDIERS** ALL OVER FLORIDA, ALABAMA & GEORGIA...

AT THE **MARCH** ON **WASHINGTON,** I WAS A **MARSHAL,** A **PEACEKEEPER.** IT WAS MY **JOB** TO MAKE SURE THINGS DIDN'T GET OUT OF HAND.

WE HAD ABOUT **2,000** PEOPLE, INCLUDING **GOLD STAR MOTHERS** — **GOLD STAR MOTHERS** ARE MOTHERS OF THOSE WHO DIED IN BATTLE.

FIRST, WE WERE SUPPOSED TO **PAY** OUR **RESPECTS** AT **ARLINGTON CEMETARY...**

WHEN WE GOT TO ARLINGTON, THEY **CLOSED** THE **GATES** AND WOULD **NOT LET** OUR **PEOPLE IN.**

PEOPLE WANTED TO **GO TO WAR** ON THE **SPOT**—THEY WANTED TO **CRASH** THE **GATES** AND **KICK** THEIR **ASSES**.

THEY TRIED TO **PROVOKE** US INTO A **CONFRONTATION**, BECAUSE HAVING **VETERANS** MARCH **AGAINST** THE **WAR** GAVE A LOT OF **STRENGTH** TO THE **ANTI-WAR** MOVEMENT.

THE POLICE TRIED TO **BREAK** OUR **FORM-ATION** & LET TRAFFIC THROUGH...

WE HAD A **CONGRESSMAN** WITH US— **PAUL McCLOSKEY**. HE WAS AN EX-MARINE & THE ONLY REPUBLICAN TO GO AGAINST **NIXON** IN '72. Mc-CLOSKEY CAME OUT & TOLD THE PO-LICE TO LET US **GO**.

WHEN WE GOT TO THE (WASHINGTON) **MALL**, THEY WERE NOT GOING TO LET US **CAMP OUT**.

THE **JUSTICE DEPARTMENT** WENT TO THE **TROUBLE** OF TAKING THIS UP TO THE **SUPREME COURT**, (WHO) RULED WE **COULD NOT** SLEEP ON THE **MALL**.

IT WAS **GUERILLA THEATER**; GUYS **LINED UP** ON THE **SUPREME COURT** STEPS, DOING THE **CAN-CAN**...

THE **POLICE** CAME & **110** PEOPLE WERE **ARRESTED**.

THEY DIDN'T **ENFORCE** THE **BAN** & THE **POLICE REFUSED** TO **BUST** US...

WE HAD PEOPLE **LOBBYING** IN **CONGRESS** EVERY DAY...

I SPOKE TO ALL THE **FLORIDA** REPRESENTATIVES **PERSONALLY**.

WE KNEW IN 'NAM THAT WHEN **CON-RESSMEN** CAME, THEY WOULD GET A TOUR BY AN **ASSHOLE** WHOSE **JOB** IT WAS TO TAKE THEM ON A TOUR TO **NOT SEE** ANYTHING **IMPORTANT**.

SENATOR **McGOVERN** ALSO HAD **HEARINGS**; I **TESTIFIED** AT HIS HEARINGS ABOUT THE WAR & WHAT OUR POLICY **REALLY** WAS...

THROWING AWAY THE **MEDALS** WAS PLANNED FOR THE **LAST DAY**.

I HAD ALL MY **MEDALS** ON ME BUT I DIDN'T KNOW IN MY HEART IF I WOULD REALLY **THROW** THEM OR NOT.

IT WAS A REALLY **HARD** THING FOR ME TO DO – ALL I HAD TO SHOW FOR **2** YEARS IN VIETNAM WAS **SHRAPNEL** IN MY BODY, **BAD** FUCKING **DREAMS**, BAD **MEMORIES** & THOSE FUCKING **MEDALS**!

I WAS GOING TO **SCHOOL** & LEARNING ABOUT THINGS LIKE **BEHAVIORAL MODIFICATION** & **POSITIVE REINFORCEMENT**... I STARTED TO SEE HOW THEY DID THAT TO ME...

ONCE I PUT **2** AND **2** TOGETHER IN MY MIND, THE **MEDALS** WERE REALLY TO-KENS TO REINFORCE **BAD BEHAVIOR**.

THE **MEDAL THROWING** WAS THE **FINAL STEP** - IT WAS LIKE CUTTING THE **UMBILICAL CORD** BETWEEN **ME** AND THE **GOVERNMENT**.

OF ALL THE THINGS WE DID THERE, IT WAS THE **HARDEST**... PEOPLE THREW AWAY THEIR **CRUTCHES**; SOME TOOK OFF THEIR **ARTIFICIAL LIMBS** AND **THREW** THEM AWAY.

WE WENT HALFWAY AROUND THE **WORLD** TO PROTECT OUR **FREEDOM** ... WHAT MAKES YOU THINK WE'RE NOT GOING TO **FIGHT** FOR IT **HERE?!**

IT DOESN'T MATTER IF IT'S THE **COMMIES** OR THE **F.B.I.** TRYING TO **TAKE AWAY** MY **RIGHTS** - I'M GONNA **FIGHT** FOR THEM.

BACK IN GAINESVILLE, WE MARCHED IN THE **HOMECOMING PARADE**... WE **KICKED ASS** IN THE PARADE!

WE WANTED TO GET THE **ATTENTION** OF THE PEOPLE OF GAINESVILLE. BUT THE **PRESS** WASN'T GOING TO **COVER** A WHOLE LOT.

IN ORDER TO GET THE **PRESS** TO COME, WE HAD TO **DO** SOMETHING **GRAPHIC**.

I BOUGHT THESE COLORED BALLS THAT YOU WOULD LIGHT & **SMOKE** WOULD COME OUT... WE CARRIED TOY M-16's BUT WE WORE **REAL BAYONETS**.

WE HAD PEOPLE STATIONED AT MAJOR INTERSECTIONS, **HIDDEN** IN THE CROWD WITH **PACKETS** OF **BLOOD** UNDER THEIR CLOTHES.

WHEN WE SAW THEM IN THE CROWD, WE WOULD **LIGHT** A **SMOKE BOMB** AND THROW IT INTO THE CROWD.

A SECOND SQUAD WOULD HAND OUT **LEAFLETS**.

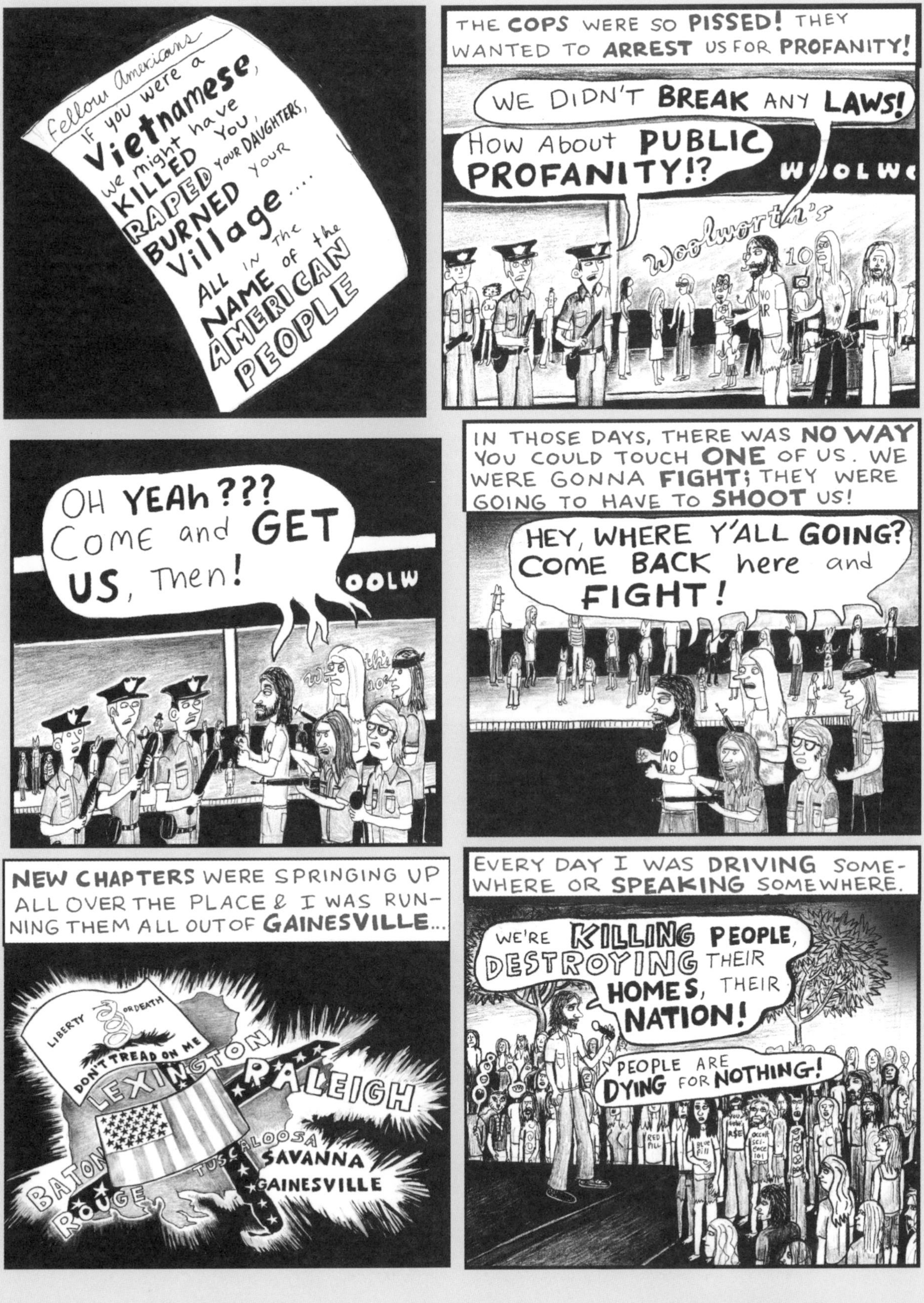

Fellow Americans
If you were a Vietnamese, we might have KILLED you, RAPED your DAUGHTERS, BURNED your Village.... ALL IN the NAME of the AMERICAN PEOPLE
THE COPS WERE SO PISSED! THEY WANTED TO ARREST US FOR PROFANITY!
WE DIDN'T BREAK ANY LAWS!
How About PUBLIC PROFANITY!?
WOOLWO
Woolworth's
OH YEAh??? Come and GET US, Then!
OOLW
IN THOSE DAYS, THERE WAS NO WAY YOU COULD TOUCH ONE OF US. WE WERE GONNA FIGHT; THEY WERE GOING TO HAVE TO SHOOT US!
HEY, WHERE Y'ALL GOING? COME BACK here and FIGHT!
NEW CHAPTERS WERE SPRINGING UP ALL OVER THE PLACE & I WAS RUNNING THEM ALL OUT OF GAINESVILLE...
LIBERTY OR DEATH
DON'T TREAD ON ME
LEXINGTON
RALEIGH
TUSCALOOSA
SAVANNA
GAINESVILLE
BATON ROUGE
EVERY DAY I WAS DRIVING SOMEWHERE OR SPEAKING SOMEWHERE.
WE'RE KILLING PEOPLE, DESTROYING THEIR HOMES, THEIR NATION!
PEOPLE ARE DYING FOR NOTHING!

I WAS ALSO GOING TO COLLEGE— IT WAS **OVERWHELMING!**

EMERSON **POE** WAS MY **BEST** FRIEND & **2ND** IN **COMMAND**...

AND WITHOUT THE HELP OF **NANCY McCOWN** & **CAROL MAZKIN**, I COULD NOT HAVE DONE **ANYTHING.**

NANCY WAS MY **GIRLFRIEND**... SHE PUT UP WITH ALL MY SHIT. I DIDN'T TREAT HER WELL; THE **WAR** HAD MADE ME **ANGRY**... I WAS **ARROGANT** & **HOSTILE.**

AND I WAS **BOSSY**... I WAS USED TO **GIVING ORDERS** -FROM MY **MARINE CORPS** TRAINING. I KNEW HOW TO **ORGANIZE** & **PLAN** MILITARILY...IT'S CALLED **BLOWBACK.**

I RENTED AN APARTMENT FOR $100 A MONTH & CONVERTED THE ATTIC INTO A **BARRACKS**...I HAD ALL THESE **HOMELESS VETERANS** SLEEPING THERE.

THEY WERE COMING **HOME** FROM **VIETNAM**, THEY DIDN'T WANT TO GO TO SCHOOL, THEY WERE BEING **FUCKED WITH** BY THE **V.A.**— SO I WAS LIKE THEIR SERGEANT.

THEY HAD TO GO TO **DEMONSTRATIONS**; THEY HAD TO **DO** SHIT.

I HAD A FUCKING **ARMY** SITTING IN THE ATTIC, SO IT WAS EASY TO GET STUFF DONE. PEOPLE WERE USED TO **FOLLOWING ORDERS**, WORKING IN **TEAMS**—SHIT LIKE THAT.

THERE WAS A LOT OF **HOSTILITY** TOWARDS US, BUT IT WASN'T BECAUSE WE WERE **VETERANS**; IT WAS BECAUSE WE WERE **ANTI-WAR**.

ACROSS THE STREET WAS THE **YOUNG AMERICANS** FOR **FREEDOM** HOUSE.

THE **YOUNG AMERICANS** FOR **FREEDOM** TURNED THEIR UPSTAIRS ROOM TO THE **F.B.I.** & THE **F.B.I.** MONITORED MY HOUSE.

THE **FIRST ARREST** WAS IN **JANUARY '72.** IT WAS FOR **KIDNAPPING** FOR **RANSOM.**

I WAS REALLY **UNHAPPY** BECAUSE I **DIDN'T KIDNAP** ANYBODY. EVERY HALF HOUR THERE WAS A **RADIO UPDATE**...

VETERANS LEADER **SCOTT CAMIL** MAY GET THE **DEATH PENALTY!**

THE NIGHT THAT I SUPPOSEDLY **KID-NAPPED** THOSE GUYS, I WAS HAVING DINNER WITH **SENATOR GRUENING** OF **ALASKA.** HE WAS DOWN FOR THE **CONCERNED DEMOCRAT CONVENTION** & I WAS THE **GUEST SPEAKER.**

Welcome! Concerned Democrats

WHEN WE CAME BACK FROM ST. PETE THIS **GUY** I KNEW FROM **HIGH SCHOOL** CAME TO THE HOUSE- HE HAD A **KID** WITH HIM & THEY **SLEPT OVER**...

I NEED ANOTHER **FAVOR**... could you **PICK UP** SOME **MONEY** for me today? I can't get over there on time...

US vs THEM duality

I WENT TO **PICK UP** THE MONEY...

I'M HERE TO **PICK UP** the **MONEY** FOR **AL!**

Sonny's BBQ Fat Boys

TAKE OUT

Here ya go... **$100**... I'll even give you a **receipt!**

$100

The Next New Thing

ON THE WAY BACK, I GOT UP TO A **STOP SIGN**...

A BUNCH OF **COPS** GOT OUT & **ARRESTED ME**.

I GOT **BONDED OUT** OF JAIL & ABOUT 20 DAYS LATER, MY HOUSE IS **RAIDED** & I'M **ARRESTED AGAIN** ON **DRUG CHARGES!**

PCP, MARIJUANA WITH INTENT TO SELL!

peace love peace love

I STARTED GETTING **CALLS** FROM **MEMBERS**,

WAR = POPULATION CONTROL

The **FEDS** went to my **PARENTS' JOBS** and told them I WAS **CONNECTED** to a **VIOLENT ORGANIZATION!** Now My Parents' JOBS are at **RISK!** I Gotta **QUIT** The **V.V.A.W.**

SO I WENT TO THE **F.B.I.** OFFICE...

COINTEL BUILDING

CHAOS CONTROL

I got a **MESSAGE** for you people... if you're gonna go to peoples' **schools** & **JOBS**, **we're** gonna go to where **YOUR KIDS** go to **school**...

tap tap tap

FEDERALLY BRAINWASHED INFORMANTS

IN **MAY '72**, WE DECIDED TO HAVE A **DEMONSTRATION** AT THE **PLAZA** OF THE **AMERICAS**. I HAD **PERMITS** TO **BLOCK** THE STREET.

WHEN THE TIME WAS **UP**, WE **UNBLOCKED** THE STREET, BUT PEOPLE DECIDED TO **STAY**.

WE TRIED TO **TALK** THEM **OUT** OF IT, BUT IT DID **NOT WORK**. RATHER THAN LETTING IT **DIE DOWN** AT ITS **OWN PACE**, THEY MADE IT A **CONFRONTATION**.

THE FIRST THING THEY DID WAS COME OUT WITH **FIRE HOSES** & **SPRAY** PEOPLE DOWN — THAT TURNED IT INTO A **CARNIVAL** ATMOSPHERE.

THE CROWD WENT FROM **250** TO **3,000**. NOW THEY HAD A **MOB**.

PLAINCLOTHES POLICE (STOOD) BEHIND THE **DEMONSTRATORS** & THREW **ROCKS** AT THE POLICE IN **UNIFORM**!

THE POLICE IN UNIFORM **CHARGED** THE **CROWD**, JUST **KICKING** THE **SHIT** OUT OF THE **STUDENTS**.

WE HAD A PRETTY **GOOD RELATIONSHIP** WITH THE POLICE, BUT WHAT HAPPENED WAS THEY BROUGHT IN POLICE FROM OUT OF TOWN—THEY WERE **REDNECKS** WHO JUST WANTED TO **BEAT** UP SOME FUCKING **HIPPIES**!

THEY HAD THEIR NAMEPLATES & BADGES **TAPED OVER**, SO WE KNEW THEY WERE GOING TO **KICK ASS** & TRY TO **GET AWAY** WITH IT.

THEY **BEAT UP** THE GODAMNED **NEWS-PAPER REPORTERS** & THAT TURNED THE PRESS **AGAINST** THEM.

THEY HIT PEOPLE WITH **TEAR GAS**—LET ME TELL YOU HOW **STUPID** THESE ASS-HOLES WERE...THEY WERE **DOWN WIND**—THE GAS **CAME BACK** ON **THEM**!

AT FIRST, I WAS A **PEACEMAKER**; THEN, I BECAME A **DEFENDER** OF THE PEOPLE.

WE WANTED TO **STOP** THEM FROM **ATTACKING** THE **STUDENTS** & DIVERT THEIR **ATTENTION** TO **US**.

WE HAD **PICTURES**... THAT NIGHT, WE WERE ABLE TO **PICK OUT WHO** WAS DOING **WHAT**; AND THEY WERE **UNDERCOVER NARCOTICS AGENTS!**

WE MADE A PLAN OF **ACTION**... WE'RE FUCKING **MARINES**, DOING WHAT WE LEARNED TO DO.

ON THE FIRST NIGHT, BEFORE WE HAD ANY **WEAPONS** OR **PLANS**, WE HAD TO USE **TACTICS**.

WE DECIDED TO SAY "**FUCK YOU**" TO THEM, & WE **SPELLED** IT OUT WITH **PEOPLE**.

WE BROKE INTO POLICE CARS - TURNING THEIR **RADIOS** ON & TAKING THEIR **HANDSETS** TO **FUCK** THEIR **COMMUNICATIONS** UP.

WE WERE HIGHLY **ORGANIZED**: WE HAD **4-MAN TEAMS** THAT WE WERE DEPLOYING TO **HOT SPOTS**.

FIRST WE HIT THEM WITH BALLOONS OF **AMMONIA**; THE AMMONIA HIT & OFF CAME THEIR **FACE SHIELDS**.

PEOPLE WILL SAY THAT THIS IS **VIOLENCE**. SURE, BUT **THEY** USED VIOLENCE **FIRST**...

WE HIT THEM **HARD** — WE PUT **18** POLICEMEN IN THE **HOSPITAL**.

400 PEOPLE WERE **ARRESTED**, BUT THEY **DIDN'T GET** ANY OF US.

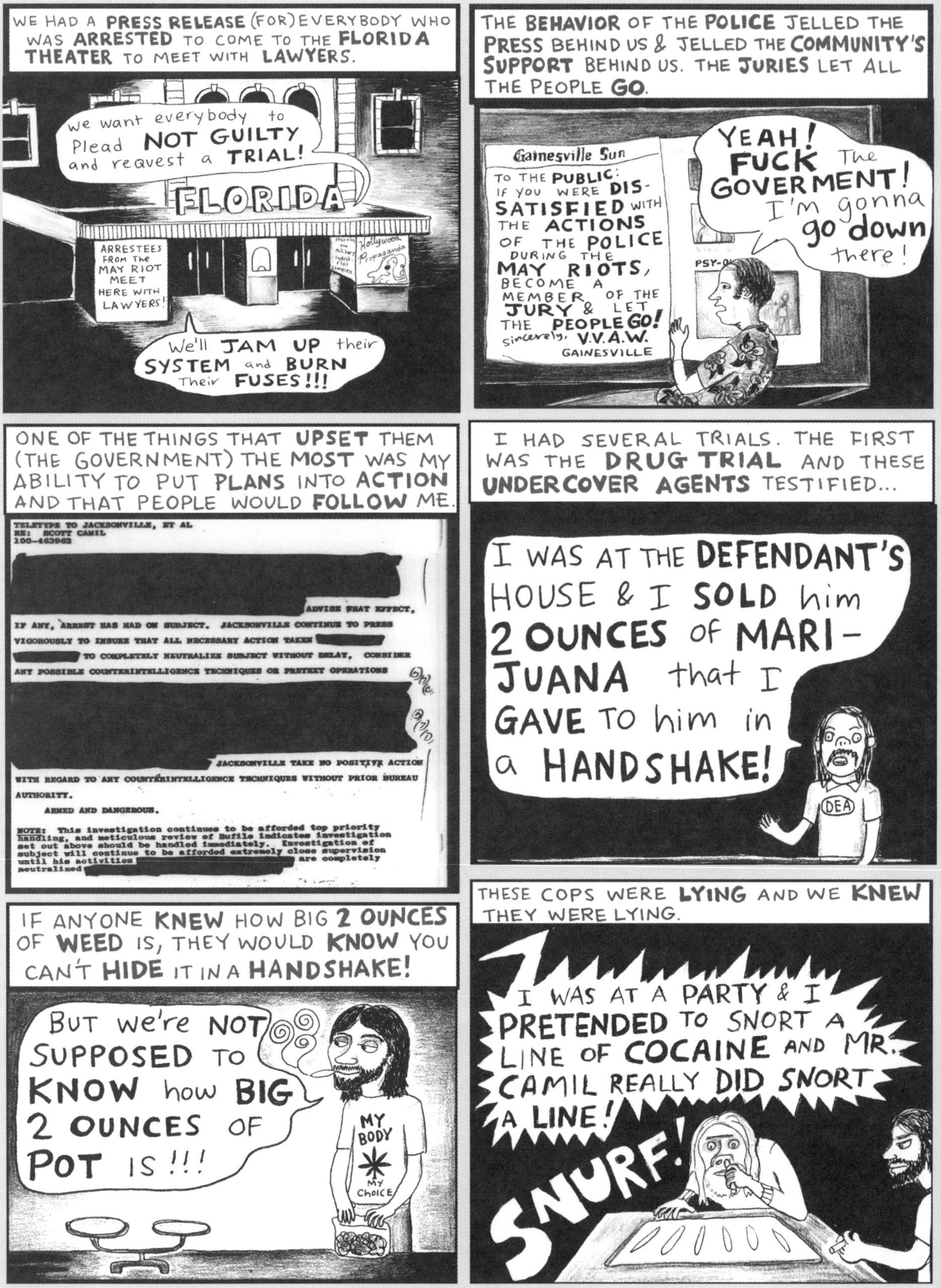

WE HAD A PRESS RELEASE (FOR) EVERYBODY WHO WAS ARRESTED TO COME TO THE FLORIDA THEATER TO MEET WITH LAWYERS.
we want everybody to Plead NOT GUILTY and request a TRIAL!
FLORIDA
ARRESTEES FROM THE MAY RIOT MEET HERE WITH LAWYERS!
Hollywood Propaganda
We'll JAM UP their SYSTEM and BURN Their FUSES!!!
THE BEHAVIOR OF THE POLICE JELLED THE PRESS BEHIND US & JELLED THE COMMUNITY'S SUPPORT BEHIND US. THE JURIES LET ALL THE PEOPLE GO.
Gainesville Sun
TO THE PUBLIC: IF YOU WERE DIS-SATISFIED WITH THE ACTIONS OF THE POLICE DURING THE MAY RIOTS, BECOME A MEMBER OF THE JURY & LET THE PEOPLE GO! sincerely, V.V.A.W. GAINESVILLE
YEAH! FUCK The GOVERMENT! I'm gonna go down there!
ONE OF THE THINGS THAT UPSET THEM (THE GOVERNMENT) THE MOST WAS MY ABILITY TO PUT PLANS INTO ACTION AND THAT PEOPLE WOULD FOLLOW ME.
TELETYPE TO JACKSONVILLE, ET AL
RE: SCOTT CAMIL
100-463962
[redacted] ADVISE WHAT EFFECT, IF ANY, ARREST HAS HAD ON SUBJECT. JACKSONVILLE CONTINUE TO PRESS VIGOROUSLY TO INSURE THAT ALL NECESSARY ACTION TAKEN [redacted] TO COMPLETELY NEUTRALIZE SUBJECT WITHOUT DELAY. CONSIDER ANY POSSIBLE COUNTERINTELLIGENCE TECHNIQUES OR PRETEXT OPERATIONS [redacted] JACKSONVILLE TAKE NO POSITIVE ACTION WITH REGARD TO ANY COUNTERINTELLIGENCE TECHNIQUES WITHOUT PRIOR BUREAU AUTHORITY.
ARMED AND DANGEROUS.
NOTE: This investigation continues to be afforded top priority handling, and meticulous review of Bufile indicates investigation set out above should be handled immediately. Investigation of subject will continue to be afforded extremely close supervision until his activities [redacted] are completely neutralized [redacted]
I HAD SEVERAL TRIALS. THE FIRST WAS THE DRUG TRIAL AND THESE UNDERCOVER AGENTS TESTIFIED...
I WAS AT THE DEFENDANT'S HOUSE & I SOLD him 2 OUNCES of MARI-JUANA that I GAVE TO him in a HANDSHAKE!
DEA
IF ANYONE KNEW HOW BIG 2 OUNCES OF WEED IS, THEY WOULD KNOW YOU CAN'T HIDE IT IN A HANDSHAKE!
BUT we're NOT SUPPOSED TO KNOW how BIG 2 OUNCES OF POT IS!!!
MY BODY MY CHOICE
THESE COPS WERE LYING AND WE KNEW THEY WERE LYING.
I WAS AT A PARTY & I PRETENDED TO SNORT A LINE OF COCAINE AND MR. CAMIL REALLY DID SNORT A LINE!
SNURF!

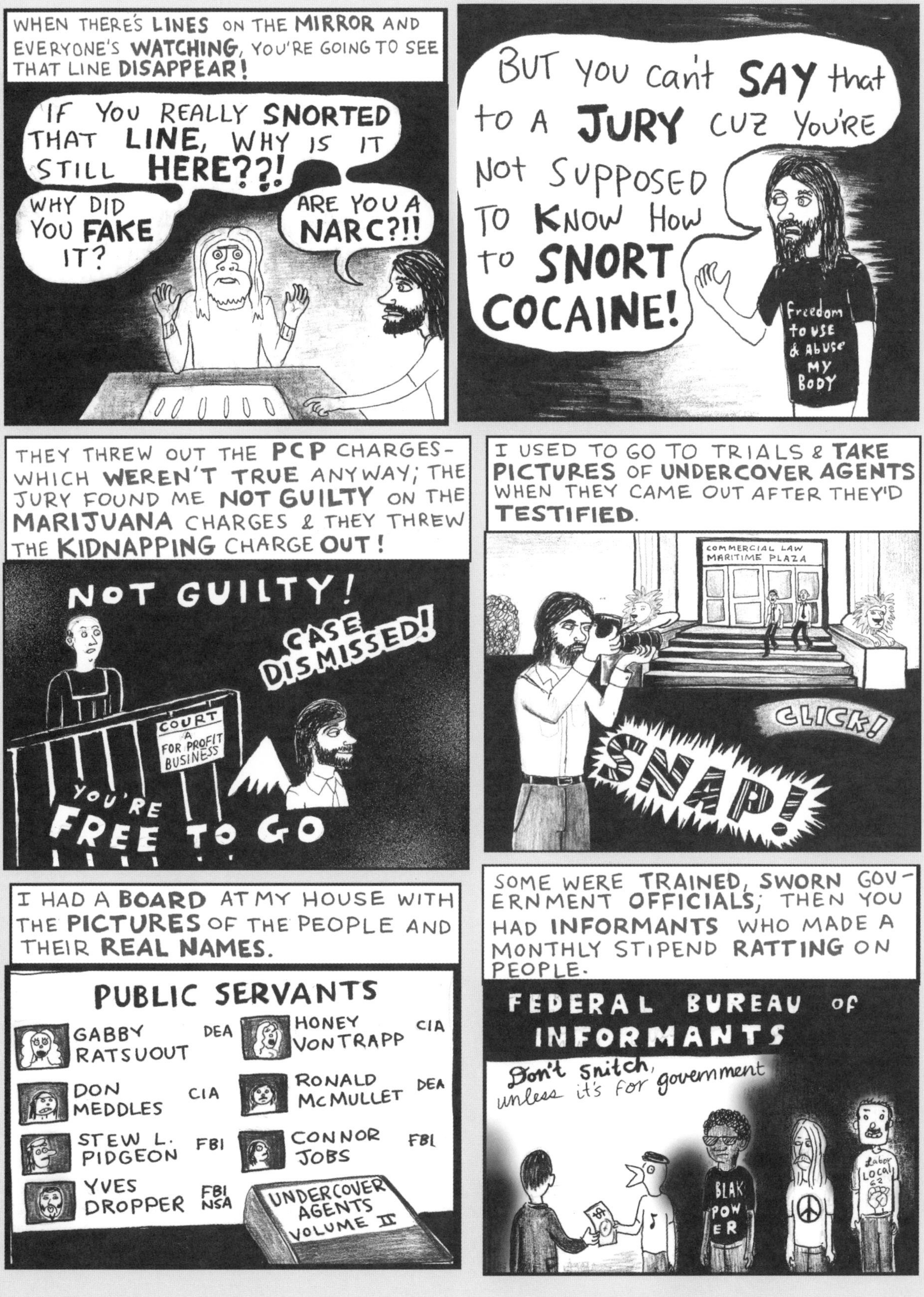
WHEN THERE'S LINES ON THE MIRROR AND EVERYONE'S WATCHING, YOU'RE GOING TO SEE THAT LINE DISAPPEAR!
IF YOU REALLY SNORTED THAT LINE, WHY IS IT STILL HERE??!
WHY DID YOU FAKE IT?
ARE YOU A NARC?!!
BUT YOU can't SAY that to A JURY CUZ YOU'RE NOT SUPPOSED TO KNOW HOW to SNORT COCAINE!
Freedom to USE & Abuse MY BODY
THEY THREW OUT THE PCP CHARGES - WHICH WEREN'T TRUE ANYWAY; THE JURY FOUND ME NOT GUILTY ON THE MARIJUANA CHARGES & THEY THREW THE KIDNAPPING CHARGE OUT!
NOT GUILTY!
CASE DISMISSED!
COURT A FOR PROFIT BUSINESS
YOU'RE FREE TO GO
I USED TO GO TO TRIALS & TAKE PICTURES OF UNDERCOVER AGENTS WHEN THEY CAME OUT AFTER THEY'D TESTIFIED.
COMMERCIAL LAW MARITIME PLAZA
CLICK!
SNAP!
I HAD A BOARD AT MY HOUSE WITH THE PICTURES OF THE PEOPLE AND THEIR REAL NAMES.
PUBLIC SERVANTS
GABBY RATSUOUT DEA
HONEY VONTRAPP CIA
DON MEDDLES CIA
RONALD McMULLET DEA
STEW L. PIDGEON FBI
CONNOR JOBS FBI
YVES DROPPER FBI NSA
UNDERCOVER AGENTS VOLUME II
SOME WERE TRAINED, SWORN GOVERNMENT OFFICIALS; THEN YOU HAD INFORMANTS WHO MADE A MONTHLY STIPEND RATTING ON PEOPLE.
FEDERAL BUREAU of INFORMANTS
Don't snitch, unless it's for government
BLAK POWER
Labor Local 62

YOU HAD GUYS WHO **NEEDED** TO **FEEL** AS IF THEY WERE DOING SOMETHING FOR THEIR **COUNTRY** & WANTED TO **GLORIFY** THEMSELVES TO THE **F.B.I.**

IN THE **GAINESVILLE** CHAPTER OF **V.V.A.W.**, OUT OF **77** MEMBERS, THERE WERE **11** DIFFERENT **AGENCIES** THAT HAD **SPIES** IN MY **GROUP!**

SOMETIMES, I'D GO TO A **MEETING** AND I'D BE THE **ONLY PERSON** WHO **WASN'T** A GOVERNMENT AGENT, AND I **DIDN'T** EVEN **KNOW** IT!

WHEN THE **DEMOCRATS** & **REPUBLICANS** DECIDED TO HAVE THEIR **CONVENTIONS** IN FLORIDA, HANDLING SECURITY BE-CAME MY RESPONSIBILITY.

WE WERE GATHERING **INTELLIGENCE**. BUT WE HAD **AGENT PROVOCATEURS** GIVING US **FALSE INTELLIGENCE** TO **ENTRAP** US IN A **CERTAIN BEHAVIOR**.

IT TURNED OUT THAT THE **COORDINATOR** FOR **ARKANSAS** WAS **F.B.I.**

THE **LOUISIANA COORDINATORS** WERE ALSO **F.B.I.**

THE **F.B.I.** WAS INVOLVED IN THE **DIRECT PLANNING** OF **EVERYTHING!**

AT THE TIME, WE THOUGHT: "THIS IS **WHAT** THEY ARE **DOING** - THEY'RE **BEAT-ING** THE **FUCK** OUTTA PEOPLE!"

IF the **GOVERNMENT** starts **WIPING** people **OUT**, we gotta get the pigs **OFF** their FUCKING **ASSES!**

WE **KNEW** THAT THE **POLICE** WOULD TRY TO **PROVOKE** US INTO **VIOLENCE** TO **DISCREDIT** US... IT WAS OUR JOB TO **NOT ALLOW** THEM TO DO THAT, BUT ALSO TO **PROTECT OURSELVES.**

SECRET POLICE

THEY **KNEW** HOW WE WERE GOING TO **REACT.** AND WE **REACTED.** AND I WROTE THE **PLANS.**

WE NEED A **PLAN** IN CASE THEY **TRY SOMETHING** AT THE **CONVENTION!**

Vets 4

Colt 43

THE PEOPLE THAT I BROUGHT IN WERE PEOPLE WHO **THOUGHT** LIKE ME...

FIRST, WE STATION **FOUR-MAN FIRE TEAMS** NEAR ALL THE **BRIDGES!**

WE'LL **SMUGGLE** IN **WEAPONS** BEFOREHAND!

Colt 43

THE WHOLE **PURPOSE** WAS **DIVERSIONARY TACTICS** SO THE FORCES WOULD HAVE TO **LEAVE** THE DEMONSTRATION TO **PROTECT** THE BUILDINGS.

IF they **RAISE** the **BRIDGES**, we'll **BLOW UP** the mechan-ism that **KEEPS** IT **RAISED** & **EVACUATE** the **WOUNDED!**

Vets against War

NO War

FUK WAR

WE WERE NOT GOING TO **INITIATE** ANY **VIOLENCE** BUT THE PLAN HAD TO INCLUDE **CONTINGENCIES** FOR **ANYTHING.**

IF they **KEEP IT UP**, we'll **FIREBOMB** the **RECRUITING STATIONS!**

The **JAILS!** the **COURTS!**

All the U.S.A. **FEDERAL BUILDINGS!**

UNTIL they **BACK OFF!**

ANY VIOLENCE ON OUR PART WOULD BE PURELY **SELF-DEFENSE.**

JUST LIKE THE **UNITED STATES** DOES NOT EXPECT **CANADA** TO **ATTACK** US, BUT WE HAVE PLANS TO **BOMB** THE **SHIT** OUT OF THEM IF THEY DO.

THE WEEKEND BEFORE THE **CONVENTION,** THEY ROUNDED UP 23 OF US FROM 7 DIFFERENT STATES...

AND **SUBPOENAED** US TO THE **GRAND JURY** IN **TALLAHASSEE.**

THEY PLANNED TO **FUCK US** AS **BAD** AS POSSIBLE—YOU COULD NOT GET A **LAWYER** ON THE **WEEKEND!**

THESE **LAWYERS** FLEW IN FROM OUT OF TOWN, INCLUDING MY LAWYER FROM GAINESVILLE, **LARRY TURNER.**

THESE LAWYERS HAD BEEN DEALING WITH THE **ABUSE** OF THE **JUDICIAL BRANCH** AGAINST THE **ANTI-WAR** MOVEMENT & THEY TAUGHT US ABOUT THE **SYSTEM**.

THE GRAND JURY
• STARTED TO PROTECT THE PEOPLE FROM GOVERNMENT
• NOW USED TO HELP GOVERNMENT SCREW THE PEOPLE

IT **PISSED** THEM OFF THAT THESE **LAWYERS** CAME IN.

BAR ASSOCIATION

WE would like a **CONTINUANCE** your honor... We don't have enough **LAWYERS** to represent everyone!

You may represent them as a **TEAM!**

YOUR HONOR, some of these men might be **UNDERCOVER AGENTS**... IF we work as a **TEAM**, IT'S NOT **FAIR** to those that **AREN'T!**

we need the **PROSECUTOR** to **TESTIFY!**

Are any of the men **SUBPOENAED** here today working **UNDERCOVER** as **GOVERNMENT AGENTS?**

NO!

Blasphemy

LATER, IT TURNED OUT THAT **3** OUT OF **23** OF US WERE **AGENTS**.

Trust us we're your friends

ALL OF US WHO WENT THERE **REFUSED** TO **ANSWER QUESTIONS**.

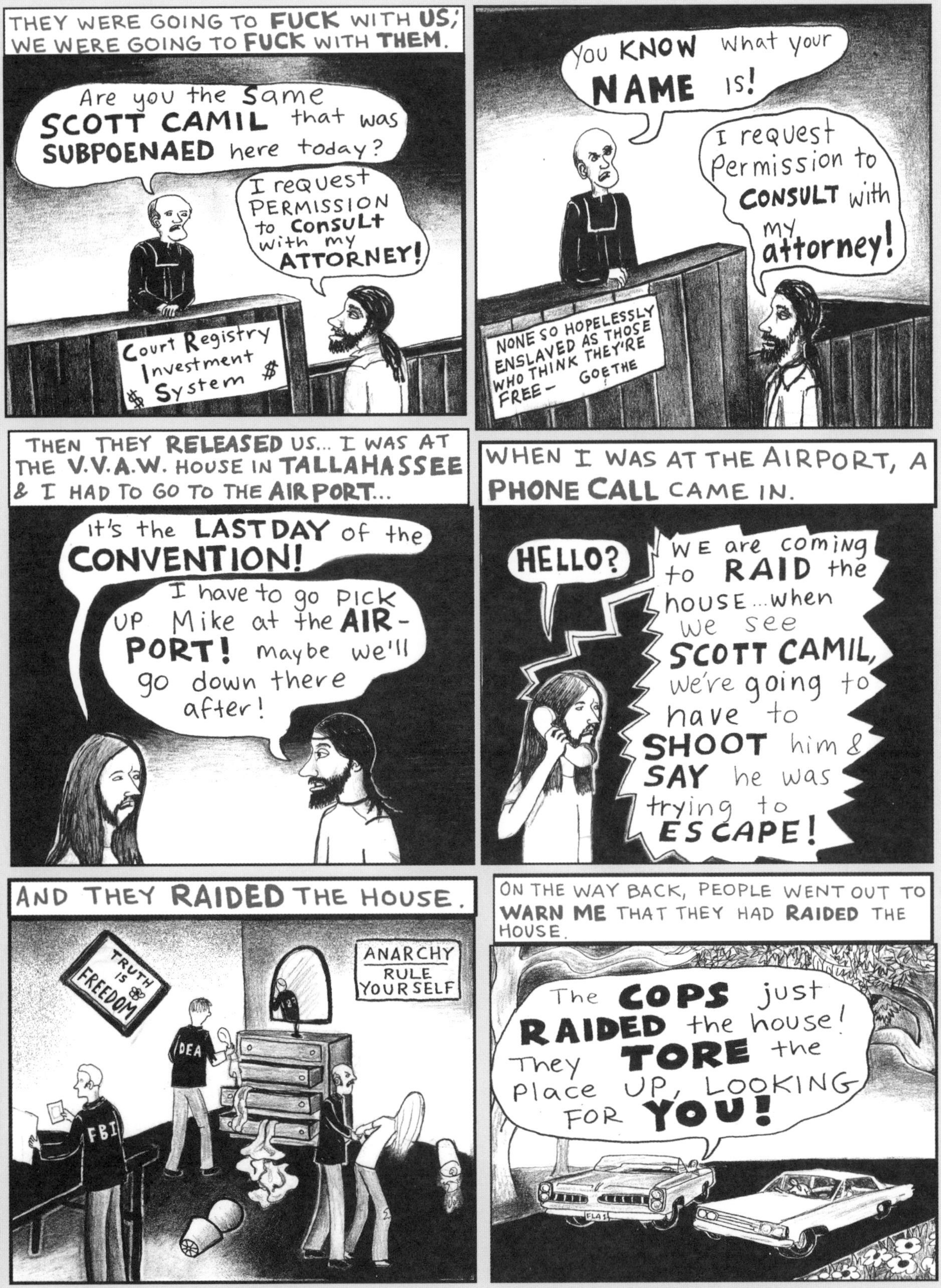
THEY WERE GOING TO FUCK WITH US; WE WERE GOING TO FUCK WITH THEM.
Are you the same SCOTT CAMIL that was SUBPOENAED here today?
I request PERMISSION to CONSULT with my ATTORNEY!
Court Registry Investment $ System $
You KNOW what your NAME is!
I request permission to CONSULT with my attorney!
NONE SO HOPELESSLY ENSLAVED AS THOSE WHO THINK THEY'RE FREE— GOETHE
THEN THEY RELEASED US... I WAS AT THE V.V.A.W. HOUSE IN TALLAHASSEE & I HAD TO GO TO THE AIRPORT...
It's the LAST DAY of the CONVENTION!
I have to go pick up Mike at the AIR-PORT! maybe we'll go down there after!
WHEN I WAS AT THE AIRPORT, A PHONE CALL CAME IN.
HELLO?
WE are coming to RAID the house...when we see SCOTT CAMIL, we're going to have to SHOOT him & SAY he was trying to ESCAPE!
AND THEY RAIDED THE HOUSE.
TRUTH IS FREEDOM
ANARCHY RULE YOURSELF
DEA
FBI
ON THE WAY BACK, PEOPLE WENT OUT TO WARN ME THAT THEY HAD RAIDED THE HOUSE.
The COPS just RAIDED the house! They TORE the place UP, LOOKING FOR YOU!

They called & **TOLD** us they're gonna say you tried to **ESCAPE** and **KILL** you! ya better **HIDE!**

DURING THIS TIME, ALL THESE PEOPLE IN **TALLAHASSEE** CAME TO OUR **AID.** THEY WERE THE LEWISES FROM **LEWIS STATE BANK** & THE SHAWS FROM **SHAW'S FURNITURE.**

AND THIS LADY, DR. **MARION HAYES**— I WENT TO HER HOUSE.

Excuse me, MRS. HAYES... I NEED A PLACE to HIDE!

IN THE MORNING, I CALLED THE **LAWYERS** AND THE **PRESS** & **TURNED MYSELF IN** AT THE **JAIL** SO THEY COULD NOT **SHOOT** ME FOR TRYING TO "**ESCAPE.**"

I'm going to **TURN MYSELF IN**, but I'm going to **DO** it somewhere **SAFE!**

STOP RESISTING!

AS WE WENT THERE, THEY **ARRESTED** SEVERAL OF US FOR **CONSPIRACY** TO **DISRUPT** THE **REPUBLICAN CONVENTION.**

LEON COUNTY JAIL

FREE THE VETERANS

WE WERE **FEDERAL PRISONERS** IN A **COUNTY** JAIL- THEY KEPT US **SEPARATED** FROM THE OTHER PRISONERS.

FROM the courts of Tallahassee

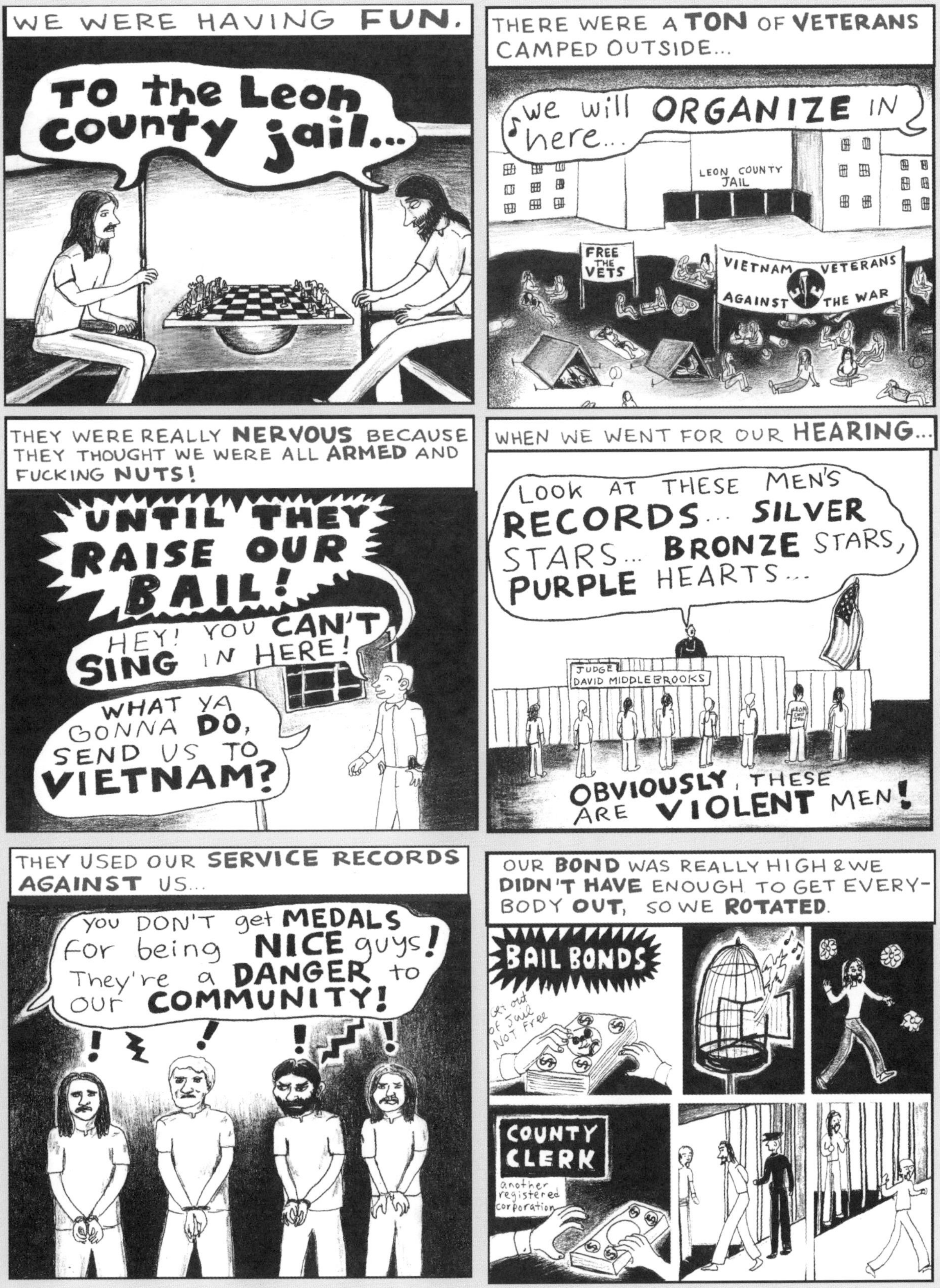

WE WERE HAVING FUN.
TO the Leon county jail...
THERE WERE A TON OF VETERANS CAMPED OUTSIDE...
we will ORGANIZE IN here...
LEON COUNTY JAIL
FREE THE VETS
VIETNAM VETERANS AGAINST THE WAR
THEY WERE REALLY NERVOUS BECAUSE THEY THOUGHT WE WERE ALL ARMED AND FUCKING NUTS!
UNTIL THEY RAISE OUR BAIL!
HEY! YOU CAN'T SING IN HERE!
WHAT YA GONNA DO, SEND US TO VIETNAM?
WHEN WE WENT FOR OUR HEARING...
LOOK AT THESE MEN'S RECORDS... SILVER STARS... BRONZE STARS, PURPLE HEARTS...
JUDGE DAVID MIDDLEBROOKS
OBVIOUSLY, THESE ARE VIOLENT MEN!
THEY USED OUR SERVICE RECORDS AGAINST US...
you DON'T get MEDALS for being NICE guys! They're a DANGER to our COMMUNITY!
OUR BOND WAS REALLY HIGH & WE DIDN'T HAVE ENOUGH TO GET EVERYBODY OUT, SO WE ROTATED.
BAIL BONDS
Get out of Jail NOT Free
COUNTY CLERK
another registered corporation

IT CREATED A LOT OF **PAPERWORK** FOR THEM SO THEY FINALLY **RE-DUCED** OUR **BOND**.

WE GOT A LOT OF **SUPPORT** FROM THE **COMMUNITY**... THE **QUAKER CHURCH** OPENED UP AN **ACCOUNT** FOR US AND WE WERE ABLE TO **GET OUT**.

WHEN WE PICKED THE **DEFENSE COMMITTEE**, WE PICKED THE PEOPLE WHO'D BEEN **SUBPOENAED** BECAUSE THEY'D **SWORN** THAT THEY **WEREN'T AGENTS**.

THE **V.V.A.W. NATIONAL OFFICE** FELT THIS WAS AN **USURPATION** OF **POWER**.

You should have **CONSULTED US** before you picked the **DEFENSE COMMITTEE**!

How do we know **YOU'RE** NOT **AGENTS**? **WE'RE** the ones going to **PRISON**!

WHEN THE **TRIAL** WAS **OVER**, WE ALL **DROPPED OUT**.

Well, we think **YOU'RE** a **C.I.A. AGENT**, Scott! **YOU'RE** the one who wanted to **FIGHT COPS & KILL SENATORS**! **YOU'RE** trying to **RUIN** the **CREDIBILITY** of the peace movement!

THE **DEFENSE COMMITTEE** HELPED US **SELECT** THE **JURY**. THOSE **12** PEOPLE **DECIDE** WHAT HAPPENS FOR THE **REST** OF YOUR **LIFE**!

MY GOVERNMENT IS NEVER WRONG!

CAN'T WE JUST CALL THEM **GUILTY** & GO HOME?

I DON'T LIKE LONG HAIRS!

IF they're here on trial, they **MUST** be **GUILTY**!

THE TRIAL WAS SET TO TAKE PLACE IN **GAINESVILLE**. IT LASTED A **MONTH** & THE GOVERNMENT PUT ON SOMETHING LIKE **28** WITNESSES.

ONCE I SAW HOW THINGS WORKED IN THE **FIRST TRIAL**, I DECIDED TO **REPRESENT MYSELF**...

IN A LOT OF WAYS, **WAR** IS **EASIER**. IN **VIETNAM**, I HAD A **GUN**; YOU FELT LIKE YOU HAD A **FIGHTING CHANCE**.

A **JUDGE** DECIDES WHAT **EVIDENCE** & **TESTIMONY** IS ALLOWED & THE **LAWYERS** GOTTA DO WHAT THE **JUDGE SAYS** 'CAUSE THEY DON'T WANT TO BE **DISBARRED**.

THE GOVERNMENT TRIED TO MAKE IT SEEM LIKE OUR **DEFENSIVE** PLANS WERE **REALLY** OUR **OFFENSIVE** PLANS!

ON THE **1ST DAY**, WE WERE GIVEN A **ROOM** AT THE **COURTHOUSE** & SOME-ONE **LOOKED** DOWN & SAW THE **FEET** IN THE **CLOSET**.

WE GOT THE MARSHALS TO UNLOCK THE DOOR & THERE WERE 2 F.B.I. AGENTS WITH BUGGING EQUIPMENT.

We're just making SURE you're not TAPPING The PHONES!

EVERY TIME THEY WERE CAUGHT DOING SOMETHING, THE JUDGE TOOK THEIR SIDE.

...AND they were RECORDING The whole meeting with our CLIENTS!

You're making a MOUNTAIN out of a MOLE-HILL!

THE FIRST WITNESS THEY CALLED WAS MY LANDLORD.

I WAS a SMALL ARMS EXPERT in the military and I saw CASES of RIFLES IN Mr. Camil's ATTIC!

Does this look like that MACHINE GUN you said you SAW in the DEFENDANT'S CLOSET?

YES, That's One of THEM!

RAT-A-TAT-TAT!

When you were in the ATTIC, Did you NOTICE That said WEAPON was BLUE & PLASTIC?

HA HA HA HA HA

I'm COLOR BLIND!

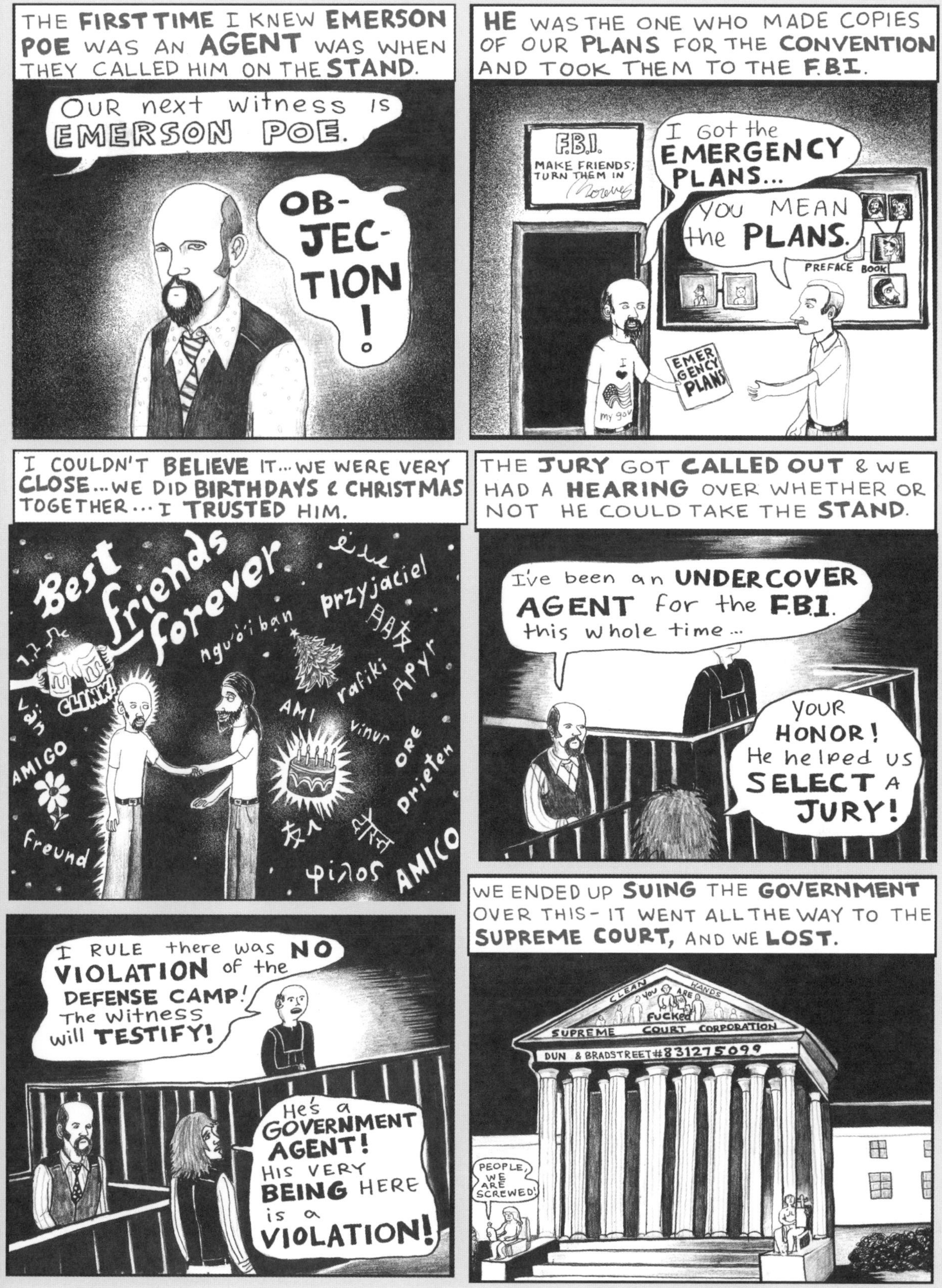
THE FIRST TIME I KNEW EMERSON POE WAS AN AGENT WAS WHEN THEY CALLED HIM ON THE STAND.
Our next witness is EMERSON POE.
OB-JEC-TION!
HE WAS THE ONE WHO MADE COPIES OF OUR PLANS FOR THE CONVENTION AND TOOK THEM TO THE F.B.I.
F.B.I. MAKE FRIENDS; TURN THEM IN
I Got the EMERGENCY PLANS...
YOU MEAN the PLANS.
PREFACE BOOK
EMERGENCY PLANS
I ♥ my gov
I COULDN'T BELIEVE IT... WE WERE VERY CLOSE... WE DID BIRTHDAYS & CHRISTMAS TOGETHER... I TRUSTED HIM.
Best friends forever
przyjaciel
người bạn
rafiki
CLINK!
AMI
vinur
ORE
AMIGO
prieten
freund
AMICO
THE JURY GOT CALLED OUT & WE HAD A HEARING OVER WHETHER OR NOT HE COULD TAKE THE STAND.
I've been an UNDERCOVER AGENT for the F.B.I. this whole time...
YOUR HONOR! He helped us SELECT A JURY!
I RULE there was NO VIOLATION of the DEFENSE CAMP! The Witness will TESTIFY!
He's a GOVERNMENT AGENT! HIS VERY BEING HERE is a VIOLATION!
WE ENDED UP SUING THE GOVERNMENT OVER THIS- IT WENT ALL THE WAY TO THE SUPREME COURT, AND WE LOST.
CLEAN HANDS
YOU ARE Fucked
SUPREME COURT CORPORATION
DUN & BRADSTREET #831275099
PEOPLE, WE ARE SCREWED!

THE **JURY** DOESN'T **KNOW** ANY OF THIS; EVERY TIME WE HAVE A **COMPLAINT**, THEY'RE TAKEN **OUT** OF THE **ROOM**.

DURING THIS PERIOD, **WATERGATE** WAS GOING ON, SO THE JUDGE **RULED** THAT THE JURY COULD **NOT KNOW** A THING ABOUT **GOVERNMENT MISCONDUCT**.

THE JURY WAS **SEQUESTERED**... WHEN THEY TALKED TO THEIR FAMILIES, **U.S. MARSHALS** LISTENED TO THEIR **CONVERSATIONS**. THEY FILED A **PETITION** AGAINST THE **COURT** BECAUSE THEY FELT LIKE THEIR **RIGHTS** WERE **VIOLATED**.

AFTER **28 DAYS**, THE GOVERNMENT **RESTED** ITS **CASE**.

THE **LAWYERS** WERE ALSO **TIRED** OF THIS **SHIT**.

NOW, WE WANTED TO **TEACH AMERICA** ABOUT THE **WAR** & WE DIDN'T HAVE THE **MONEY** TO DO **ADS** ON **T.V.**

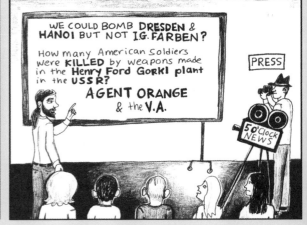

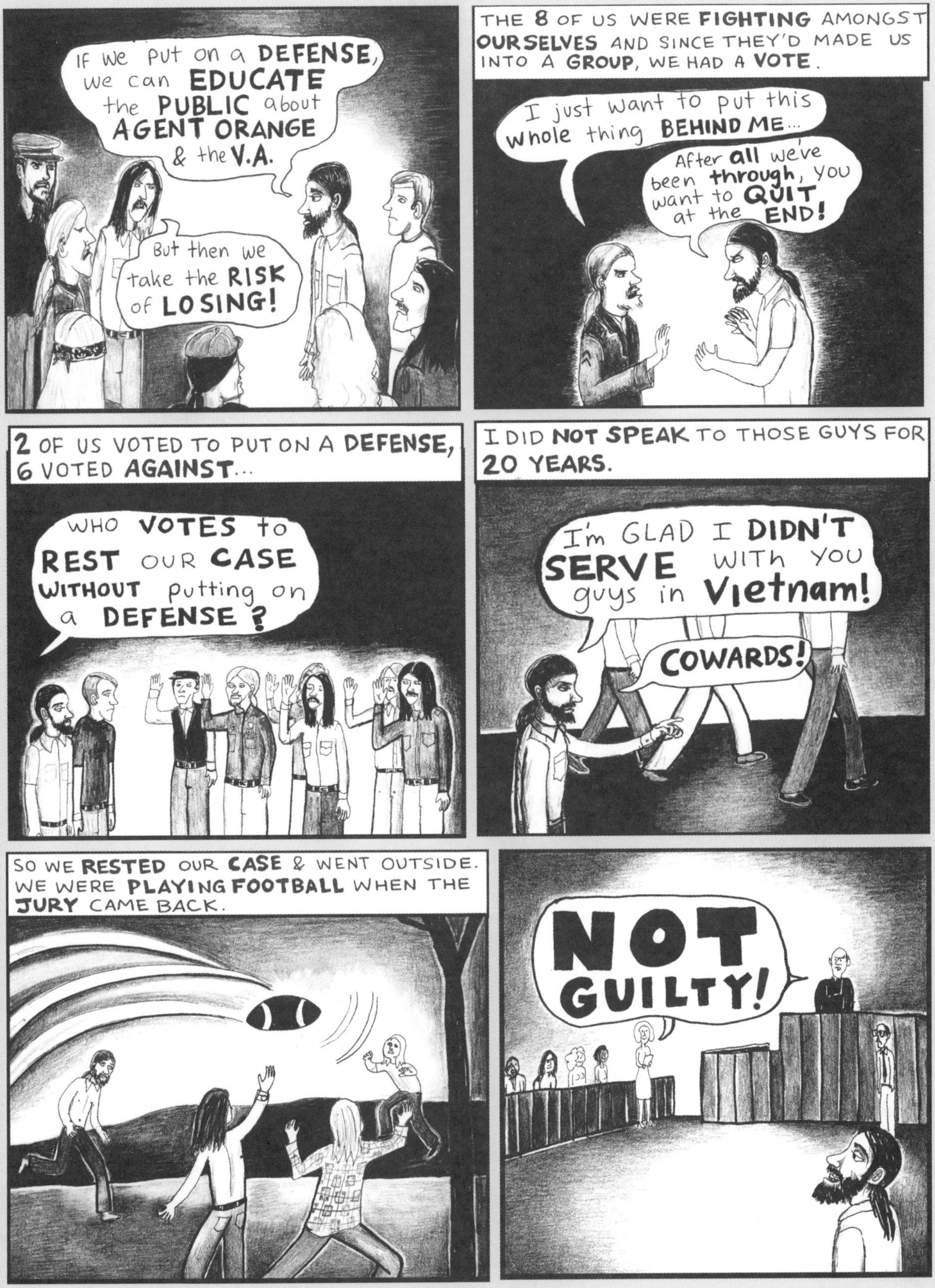

IF WE PUT ON A DEFENSE, WE CAN EDUCATE THE PUBLIC ABOUT AGENT ORANGE & THE V.A.
BUT THEN WE TAKE THE RISK OF LOSING!
THE 8 OF US WERE FIGHTING AMONGST OURSELVES AND SINCE THEY'D MADE US INTO A GROUP, WE HAD A VOTE.
I JUST WANT TO PUT THIS WHOLE THING BEHIND ME...
AFTER ALL WE'VE BEEN THROUGH, YOU WANT TO QUIT AT THE END!
2 OF US VOTED TO PUT ON A DEFENSE, 6 VOTED AGAINST...
WHO VOTES TO REST OUR CASE WITHOUT PUTTING ON A DEFENSE?
I DID NOT SPEAK TO THOSE GUYS FOR 20 YEARS.
I'M GLAD I DIDN'T SERVE WITH YOU GUYS IN VIETNAM!
COWARDS!
SO WE RESTED OUR CASE & WENT OUTSIDE. WE WERE PLAYING FOOTBALL WHEN THE JURY CAME BACK.
NOT GUILTY!

AFTERWARDS, THE **JURY** WERE **HUGGING** AND **KISSING** US—THE **F.B.I.** & **PROSECUTORS** COULDN'T FIGURE IT OUT.

you can all **LEAVE** now!

THROUGH ALL THIS, **NANCY** HAD BEEN THERE FOR ME, BUT WE **BROKE UP** BECAUSE... I'M AN **ASSHOLE**. I WISH I HADN'T BEEN SO **ANGRY**—I JUST WANTED TO **DESTROY EVERYTHING** IN MY **WAY**.

VORTEX · OF · hate · hate · hate · hate · **HATE**

I LIVED IN A TENT FOR A COUPLE MONTHS & **SNUCK** BACK INTO **GAINESVILLE**. I GOT A FRIEND TO **RENT** A **HOUSE** FOR ME SO I COULD HAVE SOME **ANONIMITY**.

SOUL UT ION

I WAS **TIRED** OF ALL THIS **SHIT**. I DIDN'T DO MOVEMENT WORK. I GOT INTO PLANTS & WAS **WRITING** A **BOOK**.

type type type type type type type type

PUBLIC SERVANTS
BOBBY SWITCHERELLI
ROY RAT ON YA
TOM TATTLER

ONE MORNING, THERE WAS A **KNOCK** AT THE DOOR, & THERE'S THIS **PRETTY GIRL**...

I'm looking for **RANDY**?

hello

HER NAME WAS **BARBARA IVES** & SHE LIVED IN **ORLANDO**.

He's not here, but you can **come inside** and **call him!**

Reefer

hello

WE SMOKED SOME **POT**, DID SOME **COCAINE** & WENT TO **BED**.

SHE STARTED COMING UP TO SPEND THE WEEKENDS WITH ME...

AND SHE **INTRODUCED** ME TO SOME OF HER **FRIENDS**.

ONE WEEKEND, THESE GUYS **CALLED** ME.

SO THEY CAME IN FROM OUT OF TOWN & WE WENT FOR A **RIDE** TO GET **DRUGS**.

I WAS SITTING IN THE SHOTGUN SEAT & THE GUY BEHIND ME **SHOVED** A **GUN** TO MY **HEAD**.

HE STARTED **HITTING** ME OVER THE **HEAD** WITH THE **GUN**...

I THOUGHT HE WAS TRYING TO **RIP ME OFF** & I WAS **NOT** GOING TO BE **COOPERATIVE**.

I **UNLOCKED** THE DOOR & WAS GOING TO **JUMP** OUT INTO **TRAFFIC**, BUT THE DRIVER HIT THE **BRAKES** & WE ALL WENT **FORWARD**.

THE GUY IN THE BACK SEAT PUT THE **GUN** UP TO MY **BACK** & **SHOT** ME.

AS SOON AS I **HIT** THE **STREET**, THIS GUY IS ON **TOP** OF ME WITH A **GUN** TO MY **HEAD**.

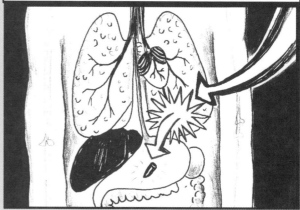

THE **BULLET** FRACTURED MY **RIB**, COLLAPSED MY **LUNG** & I LOST FOUR UNITS OF **BLOOD**. IT CAUSED **STOMACH DAMAGE** & LODGED IN MY **ABDOMEN**.

LARRY TURNER CAME TO VISIT ME IN THE HOSPITAL.

They're **RAIDING** your **PLACE!**

THE **FEDS RAIDED** MY HOUSE. THEY TOOK ALL MY **FILES**, THE **BOOK** I WAS WRITING—ALL MY **DOCUMENTATION**...

PUBLIC SERVANT
Benny Fink
Donny Ratsco

FILES

THEN, I HAD TO GO THROUGH ANOTHER **TRIAL**.

When we tried to **ARREST** MR. Camil, he **ATTACKED** US... I **HAD** to SHOOT him in **SELF-DEFENSE**.

TYRANNY IS **VOLUNTARY**

So, MY **FINGERPRINTS** weren't on the **DRUG BAGS** or the **GUN**...

The F.B.I. found **NO GUNSHOT RESIDUE** on my fingers & the **BALLISTICS** don't match your **STORY!**

TURNED OUT **BARBARA** WAS **D.E.A.** & SHE **KNEW** THE WHOLE TIME THAT THEY WERE PLANNING ON **KILLING ME**.

My wife is a friend of Barbara Ives... she told me she was **WORKING** with the **GOVERNMENT** to **KILL** Mr. Camil.

IT **HURT** ME SO BAD INSIDE, TO HAVE SOMEONE YOU THOUGHT YOU **LOVED** TRY TO **KILL** YOU.

THEY **KNEW** WHERE MY **WEAKNESS** WAS & THEY **EXPLOITED** IT.

WHEN I WENT TO THE **GRAND JURY,** THEY DID NOT **INDICT** THEM.

THIS SAME TIME, THE **VIETNAM WAR** ENDED...

WHEN THEY **SHOT** ME, THEY TOOK **EVERYTHING.** I HAD BEEN SI-LENCED. I WAS **NOT** GOING TO DO **ANTI-WAR** MOVEMENT WORK... **FUCK THAT!**

I GOT **MARRIED**, HAD **3 CHILDREN** & GOT MY COMMERCIAL **PILOT'S** LICENSE.

THEN, IN **1987**, I STARTED GETTING **CALLS** FROM GUYS I HAD KNOWN IN THE **MARINE CORPS**.

SCOTT, you have an **AIRPLANE**! Come down to **CENTRAL AMERICA** & help bring supplies down to the people!

Sorry... I'm too **OLD** for that shit!

SCOTT, they're **MASSACRING** people down here! We **NEED** your **HELP**!

I Can't! I've GOT a **WIFE** & **KIDS**!

ONE OF THE **PROBLEMS** VETERANS HAVE IS THEY **WONDER** HOW COME THEY'RE STILL **ALIVE**. SOMETHING **INSIDE** TOLD ME TO **GO**.

SO I WENT TO **CENTRAL AMERICA** ON A TRIP BEING **SPONSORED** BY **VETS** FOR **PEACE**. WHILE I WAS DOWN THERE, **EVERYTHING CHANGED**.

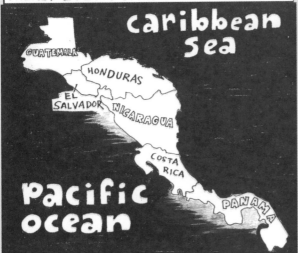

I SAW ALL THESE **CHILDREN** ON THE STREET, **BEGGING**.

IN **GUATEMALA**, WE WERE AT A REST-AURANT & THIS KID CAME IN TO **BEG**.

THE KID POURED **SALT** OVER THE **FOOD** & **RUINED** IT...

Scott, the kids here pour **SALT** all over the **FOOD** so we **can't EAT it!**

THEN MY FRIEND SCRAPED ALL THE **FOOD** INTO A DIRTY BAG.

Then they take the **FOOD** for **themselves!**

my **DINNER!**

WE FOLLOWED THE KID TO SOME **CARDBOARD** BOXES...INSIDE WAS A **LADY** WITH A **BABY** & HE BROUGHT THE FOOD TO **THEM**.

I HAD AN **EMOTIONAL BREAKDOWN** WHEN I WAS THERE, THINKING ABOUT THE CHILDREN I'D **KILLED** IN **VIETNAM**. I DECIDED I WAS GOING TO **WORK** FOR THE **CHILDREN** OF THIS WORLD.

WHY WAS I SO ROTTEN?

GUATEMALAN SOLDIERS WOULD GRAB SMALL **CHILDREN, SMASH** THEIR **HEADS** INTO TREES & **KILL** THEM TO SET AN **EXAMPLE** SO PEOPLE WOULD BE **AFRAID** TO HELP THE **GUERILLAS**.

WHAK!

THOSE SOLDIERS WERE **TRAINED** IN **FORT BENNING, GEORGIA**. OUR GOVERNMENT WAS GIVING THOSE SOLDIERS **GUNS** TO **KILL** PEOPLE WITH.

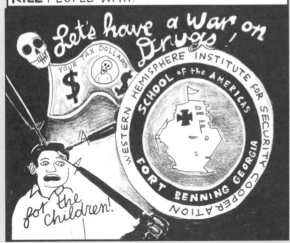

I FOUNDED THE GAINESVILLE CHAPTER OF **VETS FOR PEACE** IN 1987 IN **RESPONSE** TO **U.S. POLICY** IN CENTRAL AMERICA.

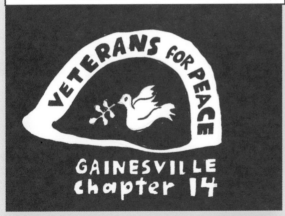

AND OUR **TAX MONEY** PAID FOR IT. WE HAVE **BLOOD** ON OUR **HANDS**.

THE NEXT THING IN MY **GROWTH** — I AM STILL GROWING — IS THAT I AM **JEWISH** & HAVE ALWAYS SUPPORTED **ISRAEL**.

SO I WENT ON THIS **TOUR** TO **ISRAEL**. I WENT TO **GAZA** & THE **WEST BANK**.

THE **PALESTINIANS** ARE TREATED **WORSE** THAN I HAD TREATED THE **VIETNAMESE** IN THE SENSE THAT THEY ARE BEING **ROBBED** OF THEIR **CULTURE**.

THEY CAN'T EVEN GROW A **TOMATO** WITHOUT A **PERMIT!**

THEY HAVE TO CARRY **PASSES** JUST TO **MOVE** AROUND.

IF THEY GET **CAUGHT** WITHOUT **IDENTIFICATION**, THEY ARE GOING TO **PRISON**.

I WENT TO **HOSPITALS** & VISITED **CHILDREN** THAT WERE **SHOT** BY **SOLDIERS**. EVERY **HOSPITAL** I VISITED, THEY WERE BRINGING IN **BLOODY, SHOT-UP** CHILDREN.

CAN YOU **IMAGINE** LITTLE CHILDREN, THROWING **ROCKS** AT SOLDIERS, **KNOWING** THEY'RE GOING TO GET **SHOT?!** THE **COURAGE** I SAW OF THE **PALESTINIANS OUTWEIGHS** THE COURAGE I'VE SEEN ANYWHERE.

NOW, IN **VETS FOR PEACE**, WE WORK WITH A GROUP CALLED **YESH GVUL**. IT'S MADE UP OF SOLDIERS WHO **REFUSE** TO GO TO **OCCUPIED TERRITORIES** & BEAT UP **PALESTINIANS. HUNDREDS** HAVE BEEN TO **PRISON.**

THE **MAIN** THING IS, I'M A **HUMAN BEING FIRST** — NOT A **JEW** OR AN **AMERICAN.** I'M **NOT** GOING TO LET **NATIONALITY** OR **RELIGION DIVIDE** ME FROM OTHER PEOPLE.

IT JUST DOESN'T MAKE **SENSE** THAT AS SOON AS IT'S **ONE NATION** VS. **ANOTHER NATION,** YOU CAN **MURDER** TO SOLVE YOUR **PROBLEMS!**

THERE'S **NO ACCOUNTABILITY** BECAUSE THERE'S **NO OUTRAGE,** AND THERE'S **NO** OUTRAGE BECAUSE THE PUBLIC IS **IGNORANT.** THEY'VE LEARNED THAT **PATRIOTISM** MEANS **BLIND OBEDIENCE** TO AUTHORITY.

IT REALLY **BUGS ME** THAT THEY'RE DOING TO **OTHER GENERATIONS** WHAT THEY DID TO **MINE.**

EVERY KID WANTS TO JOIN THE **MILITARY** BECAUSE HE THINKS IT'S **COOL,** BECAUSE IT'S BEEN **GLAMORIZED** — YOU WANT TO WIN **MEDALS** AND BE A FUCKING **HERO!**

I WENT TO **COLLEGE** UNDER THE **G.I. BILL** & TODAY ALL MY KIDS HAVE A COLLEGE DEGREE.

I GET FREE **MEDICAL CARE** AND A **DISABILITY** CHECK... I DON'T THINK IT'S ENOUGH TO **PAY** FOR MY **MENTAL SCARS.**

I LIKE THE **STRENGTH** THAT THE MARINE CORPS GAVE ME, THE **LIFE & DEATH EXPERIENCES.** IT'S MADE ME A **BETTER PERSON,** BUT AT THE **EXPENSE** OF **INNOCENT** PEOPLE.

IT JUST **SUCKS** THAT IN A COUNTRY AS **RICH** AS THE **U.S.A.,** IN ORDER TO **IMPROVE** YOURSELF, YOU HAVE TO DO SOMETHING **SHITTY!**

I'M CALLED A **TRAITOR** ALL THE TIME, BUT FOR ME IT'S **SINFUL** TO HAVE THIS KIND OF **KNOWLEDGE** AND **EXPERIENCE** WITHOUT PEOPLE LEARNING FROM IT.

FROM THE OUTSIDE, WE AT **VETS FOR PEACE** ARE A BUNCH OF **COMMIE SYMPATHIZERS** & **TERRORISTS...**

I DON'T GIVE A **FUCK** WHAT PEOPLE **THINK,** I AM STILL A **MARINE.** I'M STILL **FIGHTING** FOR WHAT IS **RIGHT.**

EPILOGUE

Vietnam trip
eve 2013

I went to Vietnam... I think it was in 2010.

I wanted to talk to the people there about the **WAR.**

Not many of the Older Viet-namese spoke **ENGLISH.**

I tried to learn some **Viet-namese** before I left, it was Pretty **ROUGH GOING...**

My favorite city in Vietnam was **HUE**, the old **IMPERIAL** **Capital.**

From there I arranged a **MOTORBIKE tour** of the **DMZ** - where **North** and **South** were once divided.

My driver could speak English & could **curse** really well... Cursing loudly, we **rode** through the jungle.

He learned to **swear** during the **war** where he was an **INTERPRETER** for the **U.S. ARMY.**

when the war was **over**, he was **left behind** to face the wrath of the **victors**...

When the North Vietnamese **won**, the people in the **A.R.V.N.**—the South Vietnamese Army—were sent to "**Re-education Camps.**"

They were told they would only be gone for a **couple** of **days**.

People spent years in those camps. My driver spent **6 years** in his camp.

When they were finally **released**, they were made to **REPORT** to the **police** every week & do free **labor** for the **local government**.

where did you go this week? who did you see? what did you do? Tell me how much you love the government!

They can be **re-arrested** at any time. Even to **TRAVEL**, they have to get **Permission**.

Can I go to Da Nang?

Why? Who are you going to see? how Long? Where are you going to stay?

Because of their **IMPERIALIST PASTS**, they continue to be kept under **surveillance**...

For years afterwards, many of them applied for **asylum** in the **U.S.A.**

Time after time, their applications were **REJECTED**.

I promised I would tell their story back home — and here it is.

Please, go home and **tell** the people about **us**!

ok!

They say that Vietnam **WON** the **WAR** — but not **ALL** the Vietnamese **WON**.

of course, in **WAR** there are **no VICTORS**...